Foolish Faith

Willie & Ann-Maria Benton

Foolish Faith

By Willie L. and Ann-Maria A. Benton

Printed in the United States of America

Book Cover Photo Credit: Zee and Jmalik Media and Photography

Ann-Maria's Hairstylist: Vizions Hair Studio, Inc.

Editing and book cover design by: Simply Ideal Solutions www.simplyidealsolutions.com.

Contents

Acknowledgements

We are so incredibly grateful for our parents. From the beginning, you've been our biggest cheerleaders. Your love, prayers, encouragement, and support never wavered and often served as the wind beneath our wings. Thank you!

We thank God for our amazing children. You are truly gifts from God. We hope to be an example of faith, unconditional love, wisdom, and encouragement to each of you. You inspire us to strive to be our best selves. May our floor be your ceiling, and may you do even greater things than us. Thank you for our beautiful grandbabies.

To our siblings and their families, thank you for your love and for having our backs. You are the true epitome of family.

To our dearest friends whom God gave the eyes to see what He was doing in and for us from day one, thank you! You displayed a foolish faith in God on our behalf and stood with and for us. Your smiles, hugs, and prayers are forever etched in our hearts.

Thank you to our church families and the precious prison volunteers who prayed us through, encouraged our hearts, and served with love: Rock Springs, Harvest, Griffin Center Point, and our TBO family.

To our incarcerated brothers and sisters who are awaiting release, we are fervently praying for you and are eagerly anticipating the day when you return to your family and community to live out your God-given purpose.

Above all, we thank God! Without Him, this book wouldn't be possible. We wouldn't be possible.

Be Inspired

But instead, God chose things the world considers foolish in order to shame those who think they are wise. And He chose things that are powerless to shame those who are powerful.

1 Corinthians 1:27 (NLT)

Super intelligent and highly gifted people are often baffled when seemingly less intelligent, less educated, or less fortunate men and women achieve great things *despite* being told what they could never do; and there is something admirable about men and women who have the audacity to believe in themselves when others do not.

There is indeed something admirable about men and women who courageously defy the laws of gravity to use their pain and disappointment as a springboard to launch themselves toward their purpose instead of allowing their situation to drag them down.

Would it surprise you to learn that God specializes in using the unassuming, the overlooked, the underestimated, and the cast aside to show off His redeeming nature and unconditional love (paraphrase of 1 Corinthians 1:27)?

All throughout the Bible, God's love, grace, mercy, forgiveness, redemptive power, and creativity are on full display through ordinary people who did extraordinary things. All throughout the Bible, God does remarkable and amazing things through ordinary people because of their *availability*, not their ability.

Remember Moses? Only God could use a stuttering murderer to free an entire nation from slavery. Similarly, He used Noah to build an ark even though it had never rained before. He instructed Elijah to lay on the body of a dead boy before bringing him back to life. And He used a young, virgin girl named Mary to carry and birth His only begotten Son, Jesus.

But get this! God did not stop with the people in the Bible. Today, we are still being inspired by individuals who overcame tragedy, refused to accept rejection, or did not allow their past mistakes to limit their future successes.

Oprah Winfrey overcame the pain of sexual molestation as a young girl to become an iconic talk show host and a wealthy businesswoman; Dr. Seuss' first book was rejected by 27 publishers before he became a beloved classic author; Tyler Perry was homeless for three months and slept in his car before becoming a revered playwriter, actor, movie producer, and studio owner; Michael Jordan didn't make his high school varsity basketball team until the 12th grade before becoming a six time NBA champion; Colonel Sanders drove around the country, sleeping in his car, knocking on doors, trying to promote his fried chicken recipe, before becoming well-known for the KFC franchise; and T.D. Jakes pastored a small congregation for years before The Potter's House became a relevant, powerful, and fruitful mega church.

Many of us are inspired by stories of people who beat the odds, overcome hardships, refuse to give up, and believe in what they bring to the table - even if they have to eat at the table alone; and eat alone, you sometimes will, when you have a vision that no one else understands or supports.

We, the Bentons, humbly add our names to the list of men and women who are walking in a promise from God. Trusting HIM despite how crazy it may have seemed, we desperately held onto a faith that appeared to be foolish to others, and we watched in amazement as God did what only He could do. We watched in amazement as God literally broke down mental, spiritual, and physical doors. We watched in amazement as God forever changed our lives and showed us that HE is REAL!

Glory be to God, He has given us an incredible story to encourage you – if He did it for us, He can do it for you! Our union seemed unlikely to some, but we knew God brought us together to set us both free.

We put our trust in Him, from day one, and this is our story, for God's glory.

Get ready to be inspired!

A Florida Christmas (December 2019)

Willie's first Christmas at home was spent in Florida. Our youngest son blessed us with a professional photoshoot for Christmas. We had so much fun. I was in my glee.

Ann

Delayed but Not Denied

We sat across the table, staring into each other's eyes. It was obvious our conversation had taken a more serious turn, becoming intense. Willie folded his arms, leaned back into his chair, and said, "It had to happen this way."

With tears in my eyes, I knew he spoke the truth. The painful truth. The difficult to digest truth.

Even though we had been praying, fasting, writing letters, and strategically reaching out to individuals for the last year, God did not answer our prayers the way we had hoped. We did not receive the good news we had been anxiously anticipating for months. And, at first, it did not make sense.

After all, *everything* had seemed to point to a glorious celebration. Beginning around January 2015, I had begun to sense a huge shift in my life. I prayed and was led to resign from my corporate career of 18 years to start my own business. Using my years of writing, editing, designing, and website developing skills, my business would help aspiring authors become self-published.

Becoming an entrepreneur was both exciting and scary since I was stepping away from all the creature comforts of working for a stable and prosperous corporation. However, God had made it painfully obvious that my time there had come to an end. I had outgrown where I was, and it was time to *grow* to a new level.

The shift did not stop there. I suddenly began to feel somewhat distant in my relationships and disconnected from my church. I was preaching and teaching around the U.S., ministering in the prisons weekly, yet there was a deep sense of *more.* Have you ever been there, *wanting* and *needing* more? There had to be more for me.

I was an empty nester. My grown sons were embarking upon their own journeys. I was living in an apartment, for the first time in almost 20 years, because of a challenging divorce and a consequential home foreclosure. The downsize from a 3,000 square foot home to an 800 square foot apartment was emotionally devastating and humbling - I was not where I thought I would be in life!

Two years earlier, in 2013, my younger son's dad and I had decided to have him complete high school in Georgia so he could experience his father's influence daily. He had been showing the signs of needing a male influence, and I had done all I could as his mom. It had been a difficult decision for me because I knew our son wanted to stay in Florida, where all his friends were, and where he appeared to have a promising future in sports.

Yes, initially, the decision was gut-wrenchingly tough! But I wanted our son to have the best shot at living out his purpose. Over the years, I visited Georgia frequently to attend his sporting events and to spend time with him.

In May 2015, he graduated high school and prepared to attend a college in another state. After the graduation, I waved good-bye to Georgia, and it was kind of strange realizing that I would not visit anymore as I had grown somewhat fond of the place. But I had no good reason to consider relocating there because my son would no longer be there.

I returned to Florida with the hope of figuring out my life, which felt like a puzzle. A puzzle that was missing a few key pieces. I felt isolated, though I was not alone, surrounded by family and friends. I felt somewhat stagnant, even though I was highly active.

The lease on my apartment would be up for renewal in November, and I had a nagging sense that I may be moving *again*. Honestly, no matter what I did, the apartment never really felt like home. However, I must admit that it was a place of transition and healing for me. It was also a place of preparation because God was up to something new.

In June 2015, I met Willie. When we initially talked, we *thought* we were connecting to discuss editing and publishing his books. Though he had already published six books, he was seeking to publish more and wanted help to enhance some of his existing book covers.

As we shared our similar love for writing, for pleasing God, and for serving others; it became abundantly clear that God was doing something much larger than a book project. It became abundantly clear that Willie was the man I had been praying for, and I was the woman he had been praying for. And guess where he lived? You got it, Georgia. The place I thought I had waved goodbye to.

Oh, did I mention that Willie was serving time in a Georgia prison?

Your reaction is probably the same as when I eventually shared with my family and close friends that God had revealed my soul mate in the most unlikely way and in the most unexpected place.

As you might imagine, they had serious concerns. Willie understood how they felt, but I will be honest and share that I was not so understanding. I was hurt by some of the responses I received. They did not know him, but they knew me; and I knew God.

Today, six years later, I can honestly say that God's hand was in everything, even the pain I experienced due to the lack of support and rejection by some. I now understand the importance of not having *everyone's* acceptance and approval when God requires us to step out in faith. God did not want me to rely upon their well-wishes. He wanted me to trust Him and *only* Him.

We cannot say that we trust God and, when the *way* He does things or allow things to unfold does not fit our expectations, we doubt. Disappointment is often the infusion our faith needs to reveal who and what we truly trust in.

I used to be a *people-pleaser.* What others thought about me, receiving people's approval, and being accepted, was a huge cornerstone of the emotional prison I was in. With that said, God has an incredible sense of humor. To free me from the disease of "what people thought," He gave me a husband whose situation made people feel a certain type of way. And I either had to get healed and get over it or stay broken and miss out on my blessing.

Do not get me wrong, the process of healing was painful to say the least. However, God brought me to a serious fork in the road early in our relationship that required me to make a tough, but necessary decision.

A few weeks after sharing with family and close friends about where Willie was and the nature of his crime, I answered the millions of questions asked and provided an opportunity for some to speak with him. What happened afterwards was extraordinary – stranger than fiction, I could not make this stuff up if I tried, I promise!

As it happened, a family member used to be "close friends" with Willie's co-defendant. Really, you must picture this: my family member was from Georgia but had moved to Florida and, 27 years later, I met the man (of all people!) who was arrested with his former close friend.

Interestingly, even though my family member had not spoken to Willie's co-defendant since he was arrested and never seized the opportunity to get the full story, he *still* felt some type of way about this guy. Strong feelings of disappointment and betrayal about another person were being interjected into *my* relationship with Willie.

My family member took it upon himself to search the internet and found *one* article about the crime and presented it to me, confronting me with what he believed was the truth, while arguing that what Willie shared with me were lies. Then came the ultimatum. If I married Willie, I would not be welcomed in their home.

For those who know me personally, you know how important family relationships are to me. This stung! It was painful, to say the least, and unthinkable!

Yet, *think* about this! Can we even call it a coincidence? Absolutely not! As Christians, we must recognize that when God goes out of His way like *this*, He wants to do something powerful – this was Him for sure.

When I spoke with Willie after the hurtful conversation with my family member, he provided at least eight other articles from the incident. And guess what? Each article was *spun* according to the targeted audience. And buried amidst all the angles of each article was a truth that could only be revealed by *one* person, Willie, the one person who knew everything. But my family member refused to speak with Willie.

I cannot stress how patient and understanding Willie was. Explaining how there were probably only one or two people he had met while incarcerated that he would introduce to his family, he said he would not be upset or disappointed if I decided to walk away. No, he would honor my decision and wish me the best.

Cleary, I had a tough decision to make that required hearing directly from God. In that hurtful moment, I felt like I was being forced to choose between Willie and my family. But the truth is, I was choosing between people and my promise. I was choosing between what people were saying and what God was doing.

When I saw it this way, I realized it was not a difficult choice at all. I chose God! More importantly, I chose everything He had for me, especially Willie, even if no one else understood it or liked it.

To this day, we cannot attest to what God wanted to do in our family member's life. Perhaps extend grace, mercy, and forgiveness with an opportunity to mend a once close friendship that has been broken for over thirty years. Maybe God was providing an opportunity for healing and closure.

Regardless of what God was doing with them, we are confident about what He was doing for us. This was my moment. It *had* to happen that way. I had to be placed in that uncomfortable situation because God was, once and for all, freeing me from the need of people's approval and the fear of rejection. It was time!

Over six years later, most of the people who doubted, questioned, or drew conclusions back then, have come around. And I am confident it is because Willie and I have been consistently obeying God and the fruit in our lives is evident, reminding me of when Jesus spoke a special blessing among those who would believe He is the Risen King without seeing Him or touching His body. For it is definitely easier to believe after the fact than it is to have a foolish faith.

Although that situation was painful, I learned a valuable lesson: Sometimes, we want to invite people into a place of faith that they simply cannot go. They are unable or unwilling to see what God is doing, and that is okay. We must guard against becoming offended, or taking it personal, like I did. And we cannot try to force people to see what we see. More accurately, we cannot make people see what God is showing us.

I realize now that some were not equipped to embark upon our journey - they would have been distractions. God had to surround us with *believers* whose faith (in God) was just as foolish, just as ridiculous, just as box-shattering, and just as unconventional as ours.

It was our leap of faith, not theirs.

When God revealed that Willie was the final puzzle piece, I did what some perceived as totally foolish! I strapped on my heels and chased after what God had for me. I packed up my stuff and relocated to Georgia when my lease expired in November even though, at this point, I had only known Willie for about five months.

The relocation was effortless because God provided for my *every* need. That is how we know it is Him. When He shows us the vision, He also provides for it (pro-vision).

I will admit that the first year or so in Georgia was rough because, even though I chose to pursue my purpose, I still reminisced on the people at times. Human nature is such a complicated thing. For a while, rather than focus on who was with me, I lamented on who was not; and that is what kept me feeling down on some days.

If you are currently in a season of transition, do not dwell on where you were. Focus on where you are going. Where God is taking you is better. But you cannot enter a new season with one foot firmly planted in the old one.

As you read this, I want to encourage you - it is not too late. You are not too young or too old. Your past mistakes are not disqualifiers for God. In fact, your brokenness and humility are the very things that qualify you for God to do the extraordinary through you and for you! Your lessons learned and the obstacles you overcame are the very things that equipped you to be used in a mighty way, for His glory!

So, go back to school, apply for that job, start that business, relocate, write that book, etc. Step out of the boat; and whatever you do, keep your eyes on God.

While there may be many reasons why you think you should not, there will always be *one* reason why you should – having *foolish* faith in God!

When I first met Ann, I was truly a happy bachelor. Seriously! I was not looking for a wife, and I did not need anyone to “hold me down” as I served my time. I was unattached, independent, doing my thing and doing it well.

While she was definitely the woman I had prayed for years ago, there had come a time when I stopped focusing on my own desires and began concentrating on what God chose me and called me to do. There came a time when I made a conscious decision to use my gifts and talents to be a blessing to others instead of pursuing wealth and fame. More precisely, I made a conscious decision to become an inspirational writer and a motivational speaker instead of an urban novelist.

Thinking back, I cannot help but smile; because, when I went to prison at age 17, I did not *know* God. I did not want to *hear* anything about Him, and you could not tell me *nothing*. Straight up!

Sadly, I was young, stubborn, and ignorant; yet I thought I knew everything, like most teenagers. I thought I was grown, and I believed I was invincible. I was already married, and we had a one-year-old son. Believing I was doing what was needed to provide for my family, lying to myself, I became involved with selling drugs. One bad decision led to another, and before I knew it, I found myself in the middle of a life-changing altercation. I found myself doing the unthinkable, taking the lives of two people who didn't deserve to die.

Truth is, I deserved to go to prison and doing so saved my life. And while I took advantage of everything offered to me, the most important thing I did was give my life to Jesus.

Another important thing I did was use my God-given gift of writing to facilitate my healing, deliverance, and spiritual growth. For writing allowed me to explore and express my deepest regrets, hurts, fears, concerns, and dreams. And the deeper my relationship with Jesus became, the more His influence in my life began to bleed into my writing; and I began writing inspirational fictional stories to uplift, encourage, educate, and entertain.

As Ann said, when we connected, I had already established my own publishing company and had published six books. Since her business was geared toward helping authors, we initially enjoyed a deep and meaningful conversation about things few people could relate to, and it did not take long for us to realize that we were the answer to each other's prayers.

When she shared what God had been doing in her life, we realized that Georgia was her Promised Land. She had fulfilled her potential where she was, and God wanted to take her to the next level. He was ready to promote her, and she had to decide if she was truly ready to take the next giant step. She had to decide if she was willing to seek first His Kingdom and His righteousness, trusting that everything else would be added onto her (Matthew 6:33).

I believe a lot of people *thought* she was moving to Georgia because of li'l ole me. But God had started preparing her heart for Georgia before He connected us. So, it was bigger than me. It, in fact, it was bigger than her because it was about her purpose and her destiny. While I am a part of it, Ann was not being committed to our cause, she was being obedient to her calling.

Unfortunately, the first six months or so were rough for her; and my heart broke for her because of the amount of pain she was in, feeling abandoned and rejected by people she loved. People she expected to be there for her. However, though I sympathized, I did not stress it because I knew God, and I knew myself.

Yes, I *knew* God! So, I assured Ann there was no way the God we serve would give her the man she prayed for and allow her to lose the ones she loved in the process. That is not how God works - He blesses our obedience, and Ann was obedient.

I also knew *myself*! That is why I often expressed how "happy!" I was for her that God had chosen me for her. My statement was not one of arrogance, it was one of "Godfidence." I knew who I was in the Lord. I knew what God had done in me, and I knew who He created me to be. My identity was not in my situation, it was in God. I knew my heart, and I knew my honorable intentions.

Ann is an anointed, loving, and faithful woman. She is wise, discerning, and incredibly strong. An overcomer, she was a gift from God; and I was being entrusted by Him to love, cherish, honor, respect, and keep her safe. She was, is, and always will be God's daughter before she's my wife. And that is something I took and will always take seriously.

Understand something, I am not a man who plays games. However, sadly, I cannot say the same for every person who is incarcerated. So, I understood why some had legitimate concerns. Really, I got it! And if it had been my mother, my sister, or my daughter, I'm sure I would've felt some type of way.

Especially since Ann is an incredibly special woman. There are so many things to admire about her, but one of her most cherished qualities is her loyalty. During a time when most people had forgotten about me, she jumped into the fire with me. For that, I will be forever grateful.

Ann's disappointment was in the people who were not ready to know me, people who simply needed time. Rather than give them the time they needed, she tried hard to convince them at first. More accurately, she tried to do God's job. In doing so, she often made things harder for herself.

As for me, I did not want people to trust me or trust Ann. No, I prayed for people to trust what God was doing. I wanted people to have the ears to hear and the eyes to see that God was perfectly aligning things in our lives to facilitate our mental, spiritual, and physical deliverance. After all, it was so obvious to us that He was doing something BIG.

Prior to meeting Ann, I had been denied parole four times over a period of eight years even though I had already done everything above and beyond what was expected of me and required by law. Each time I was denied parole, two years were added to my sentence – that is, I was "set off" for two years.

My record was impeccable, and I was entrusted with duties that displayed an ability to be trusted; and yet, for years, the only reason cited for denial was the improperly considered immutable "nature and circumstances" of the crime I committed twenty plus years ago.

When we met in June 2015, I was coming up for parole for the fifth time in May 2016. We genuinely believed, because of the way things were lining up, this had to be the year of release. Especially since God had blessed me with my soul mate, His precious daughter, who had stepped out in faith by moving to Georgia to prepare a lovely home for us. Not to mention that we were doing great things together for the Kingdom, combining our knowledge, skills, and resources to be a blessing to others.

We fasted and prayed, wrote letters to the parole board and other officials, and did everything within our power. Still, much to our dismay, they set me off another two years. By this time, I had served 28 years, and they wanted me to do at least 30 years.

It was disappointing to say the least, and it did not make sense until Ann and I were having a revealing conversation during visitation a few weeks later. After listening to her share a few things, I realized a simple truth:

"It had to happen this way," I told her, because God was still preparing us to receive and appreciate the enormous blessings He had in store for us.

At that time, she did not realize it, but Ann was not comfortable with where I was. She was low-key ashamed or embarrassed, so she hid it and figured I would be released and, therefore, could avoid having to "talk about it."

Needless to say, the set off was a game changer, and we were forced to deal with some tough questions. First and foremost, we had to decide where to go from there. You see, it was easy to plan for a wedding and a honeymoon and a future when it appeared I was about to be released from prison, but now... Could our relationship survive the two years? And what if I was not released in two years, or five years, or ever?

Much to her credit, Ann never wavered in her decision to jump into the fire with me, even when the heat was turned up. She never second-guessed us, believing more than ever that I was the man for her, even if I never left prison alive. She vowed to be with me and to love me no matter where I was. And I watched in amazement as God gave her the boldness to speak with honesty and transparency about our relationship, inspiring many.

I, in turn, grew to love, admire, cherish, honor, and respect her on a-whole-other level, to the heavens and back. You see, loyalty and devotion are two of the most important attributes to me – if you are down for me, I will be down for whatever with you!

Understand something, if I had not been set off, I would not have known if Ann was attaching herself to my upcoming release and subsequent promises, or if she was truly attaching herself to me, to our destiny. And because of what God was doing, this was particularly important to me.

So, in my eyes, if the set off was a test, Ann aced it! And I would forever be grateful. More precisely, I would marry her and give her all the love, happiness, and success she deserved; I would trust her completely with my heart and devote myself to her, giving all of myself to her and our purpose, simply because she deserved nothing less.

We will share more about what God did during our time of delay – a much needed delay. Yes, it was needed for Ann, but God did amazing things in and through me during that time as well.

It was a delay for development.

As Ann shared, she still needed to heal and be released from people's approval, acceptance, and understanding. As for me, God wanted me to increase my service to Him, to have a larger impact on the lives of the men around me (older and younger) before I left.

God did not say, "No." He just said, "Not yet."

It is *our* prayer that our story will help you to recognize God's hand in your life. Do not be discouraged or deterred from what you are believing God for. Just because it has not happened, does not mean it won't. Know that His delay is not a denial. Keep trusting the process and hold on tight to the promise He spoke to your heart.

Happily Engaged (September 2015)

This was our very first photo together. We had an inkling that we would look great together and this photo proved us right.

Built to Last

He is like a man who chooses the right place to build a house and then lays a deep and secure foundation. When the storms and floods rage against that house, it continues to stand strong and unshaken through the tempest, for it has been wisely built on the right foundation.

Luke 6:48 (TPT)

Ann

I love the above Scripture. It says, prior to building a house, we must choose the right place to lay the foundation. No one would knowingly build a house on a weak or unstable ground. Yet, when it comes to relationships, we sometimes try to bypass establishing a firm foundation and hope it can stand when tested.

For years, prior to meeting Willie, I tried to build meaningful relationships (including two marriages) on foundations that were not solid. Some relationships were established on emotions, to meet needs, or to escape. Some were the result of simply moving too fast. Because I had no true sense of my identity and self-worth, I hoped that attaching myself to the right person would help me find it. In other words, I was looking for others to define my worth.

Since I was a well-known minister who was traveling, preaching, teaching, and helping others heal, those in my inner circle thought my life was hunky dory. But deep down, I was lonely and feeling unfulfilled because I did not have a husband to share my life with. Although I had experienced being divorced, I still believed in marriage. And I still believed in my God-given soulmate.

Problem was, not knowing who I was made it easy to seek what I *wanted* in a mate, while never considering what I *needed.*

Fortunately, at 47, something clicked. I eventually became tired of the pain associated with ending relationships after deeply connecting myself to the wrong people - it takes too much work to try to make the wrong thing the right thing. If you spend most of the relationship trying to change the other person into who you want or think they should be, that is not your person. I have learned that relationships *take* work, but they shouldn't *be* work!

Throwing my hands up, I prayed some more, had been praying for years, asking God to send me the right man. Then one fateful day, He revealed that I needed to first focus on becoming the right woman. Ouch!

Knowing that He was right, conceding that I definitely needed to do something different, I made a radical decision: I chose to become celibate until however long it took for God to send the man He has for me. Being celibate (abstaining from sex) is not a new concept, but it is an underestimated one.

Being celibate is not just a "no sex" thing. It is a different kind of fast, an emotional and physical detox that helps us place things in the proper perspective. You see, sex in a relationship (outside of marriage) can become a major distraction, and it can cause us to *think* a relationship is more serious or further along than it really is because the physical intimacy is hot and steamy.

Sadly, sex is the shaky and uncertain foundation many try to build their relationships on. However, physical intimacy should be viewed as the icing on the cake. It makes the cake a bit tastier; but, without it, the cake is still a cake. That is why we need to take the time to bake the cake in our relationship with all the much-needed ingredients: affection, communication, honesty, trust, faithfulness, loyalty, commitment, and respect, etc.

I learned some hard lessons about these things as a teenager, when someone I trusted violated me sexually and *stole* my virginity. While I did not consent, crying and begging him not to do it, I could not stop him; and for years, I incorrectly blamed myself for being at his home in the first place.

Worse, my irrational but unshakable sense of deserving what I got led to a promiscuous mentality and set me up for failed relationships that were established on sex. Even though I was looking for love.

As an adult, no longer promiscuous, but deeply desiring a meaningful connection with someone, the notion of sex being the most pivotal part of a relationship became a cornerstone belief. Sadly, I did not know how to love myself, so I hoped to find someone who would love me. And, quite frankly, that had not been working out too well.

So, as you can imagine, deciding to become celibate facilitated an important time of healing and rediscovery of myself through the eyes of God. However, the most significant part of it was the agreement I had made with Him, vowing that the next time I was going to be physically intimate would be with my new, heaven-sent husband - I even had the audacity to pray, if it were not asking too much, that my husband would also be celibate.

Now, this was three years *before* I met Willie, and I had practically given up the preoccupation of *looking* for a husband, focusing on ways to help and serve others instead. In doing so, I became stronger and more resolved to remain pure as each month and each year went by, thinking nothing of it.

Then, when I was not expecting him, came Willie. And while many might think that falling in love with a man in prison might be the worst thing ever, it turned out to be the best thing that could have ever happened to me.

Remember when I noted how God has a sense of humor? And remember how I prayed for my heaven-sent husband to be celibate? Well, because of my true desire to keep that covenant with God; He not only helped me honor and protect my promise, but God also did exceedingly and abundantly above what I asked by blessing me with a man who had been celibate for at least *twenty-eight years!*

As it happened, where Willie was being housed allowed us the undistracted time needed to lay an incredibly solid foundation, to really get to know each other. So, when we said, "I love you," sex had nothing to do with our feelings for each other.

Do not get me wrong, we were very much attracted to each other - my husband is fyinnne y'all! But our attraction for each other was so much deeper. We were attracted mentally, through our various stimulating conversations. We were attracted spiritually, through sharing our love for God, constantly praying together. And we were attracted emotionally – we loved to be in each other's presence.

I remember the day Willie said, "I like you." And I thought: *Well, of course you do.* Then he explained that while many people love each other, it is another thing to really like someone. Like whom they are. Like their presence. Like their conversation. Like spending time with them - we would sit and talk for five to six hours during visitation every Saturday, then do it again on Sunday.

We were baking our cake, taking the time to add all the necessary ingredients. And when the day would come for us to be physically intimate, we believed the icing would be delicious. But until then, the cake was able to establish and retain its value without it.

This was important for me! I needed to experience a love that had nothing to do with my sexuality; and I had to unlearn the lies I believed, to undo the unhealthy patterns established in my life.

You might be reading this and think to yourself: *That's just a coincidence.* No! That is God's response to a prayer that would seem foolish to others but dripping in faith for me. That is God honoring my obedience. And that's God doing what was best for me, knowing what I needed more than I did.

After discussing it honestly, Willie and I acknowledged that had we met after he was released, things probably would have gone one of two ways: Either I would have broken my covenant with God, reverting to my old ways, and had sex with Willie before we were married. Or, we would have tried to honor my covenant with God by getting married too quickly, without taking the time to establish our foundation. But God! He was determined to help me keep my promise, by giving me the man positioned to help me honor and respect my covenant.

For this reason, we must know that who/what God has for us, is for us. No need to force or rush relationships. Give yourself the time needed to build something that will withstand the test of time. Seasons change, but a firm foundation remains intact through each one.

I am a carpenter by trade, so I understand the importance of having a firm and solid foundation. I also know the difference between something that *looks* good and sturdy from something which *is* beautiful and durable. Take furniture made from "press-wood," for example. The name says it all – it is literally saw dust pressed down, glued together, and covered with a nice-looking veneer (finish tape).

No doubt, press-wood is relatively inexpensive, and it really can look nice; but it can never compare to something made from natural (God made) hardwoods like oak, maple, pecan, etc. In fact, it is not built to stand the test of time – move the furniture piece more than once and it will probably fall apart.

Knowing this, I am always surprised by the number of people willing to pay millions for the beach front condo with a killer view and *fake* kitchen cabinets. Similarly, I am shocked by the number of people who commit to long-term relationships for the wrong reasons, before they get to know who they are connecting themselves to – I thought I was the only young fool to do that.

Prior to meeting Ann, I do not know if I considered myself celibate, because it was not entirely by choice – that is, I didn't knowingly and willingly vow celibacy. Nevertheless, after getting to know her, her past, and her desire to honor God with her life; it became apparent why it was important for me to have kept myself pure and unattached over the years.

If I had been a guy with emotional or other types of unhealthy attachments with women, I would have been a stumbling block to her healing. So, I thank God that He was able to use me, because I was naturally inclined to treat Ann like the remarkable and amazing daughter of the Most High God she is.

Still, as we got to know each other, it became obvious Ann was waiting for the veneer to fade away to reveal the press-wood. It became obvious she was struggling with the notion of me loving her for who she is rather than what she could do for me. Sadly, there were even times in the beginning when she would share an ugly part of her past with me, believing I would reject her after learning about it – as God would have it though, I had my own issues and was in no position to cast any stones at her or anyone else!

Nothing she ever told me could alter who I *knew* her to be. Nothing she ever told me could diminish what I saw in her and understood about her purpose. Nothing she ever shared with me could make me love her any less, and she eventually got it when my adoration did not change. She finally acknowledged it when I continued to affirm her value and her worth. After all, this was the woman who had jumped into the fire with me, and we would endure *anything* and *everything* together.

Overcoming the stumbling blocks in her mind, one of my goals with Ann was to help her understand my desire to make love to her all day, *every* day. Not just physically, but emotionally, mentally, and spiritually. And certainly not because I wanted something in return. No, I wanted to develop such a deep intimacy with her that, if I never physically touched her, she would feel wanted, loved, and appreciated.

At first, she did not understand this concept, but she eventually grasped it because of the affectionate and respectful way I treated her. After all, while my mouth could speak a million wonderful words a minute, my actions always spoke louder and faster. Thus, the way I treated her, the way we honor and appreciate each other as a gift from heaven, helped establish a solid foundation for our relationship.

Of significant note, we must point out how God was not only in the midst of our budding relationship, but also how His impeccable timing allowed for it all to work together for our good. You see, had I met Ann 20, 10, or 5 five years earlier, none of the interaction needed for the healthy development of our relationship would have been available since the only form of communication would have been through fifteen-minute collect calls and hand-written letters.

Nevertheless, by the time we met, inmates had access to email and video calls. More importantly, as it happened for us, I was in a minimum-security prison that allowed weekly visits. And it was during those visits, which were like supervised dates, that Ann and I really got to know each other and discover God was truly doing something astounding. It was during those up close and personal visits that my actions spoke louder than my words, allowing Ann to witness my sincerity.

As we write this book, we have been together almost six years, and the storms have hit. The winds have howled. The rain has fallen. But we are still standing. We have weathered the seasons together. We have experienced the barrenness of winter, the scorching summer sun, the falling away of autumn leaves, and the blossoming excitement of spring.

It is particularly important to get to know and see someone in *all* seasons, because you need to experience them at their best, as well as their worst. You want to experience their laughter *and* their tears.

And you want to be there for the victories and the defeats.

The various seasons of life not only reveal who the other person truly is, but also exposes who we are in the process.

After a relationship has weathered the various seasons and is able to stand the test of time, we can know, with confidence, that we have found God's person for us. We can know for certain that the person is truly for us, believing in us, loving us as we are, for who we, the same way Our Father loves us.

No question, Ann was meant to be my beautiful wife, my help mate, my soulmate, and my best friend. For that reason, not long after the two-year set off, we were happily married while I was still incarcerated.

And get this, we chose the date of my initial arrest to reclaim it and redeem it, as a reminder that God was doing something new, something special. For with Ann, God has given me a *new* life sentence, and I gladly serve it with her by my side.

We are the #BentonsforLife.

It is *our* prayer that if you are married, you will cherish the person God has blessed you with. Never take them for granted. Allow them the grace and space to grow. Do all you can to grow together and not grow apart.

If you are single, it is our prayer that you will trust God to mature you into the man/woman who is ready to be a blessing to the person He has for you. Do not be impatient. Good people are born, but great people are developed over time.

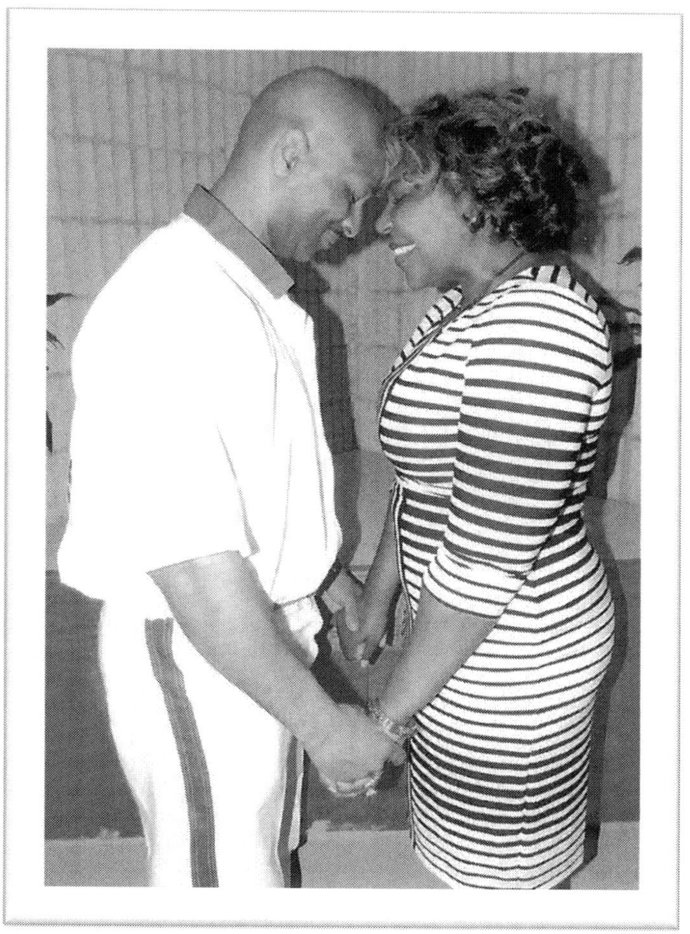

Our Wedding Day (January 2017)

For better or worse, 'til death do us part. Like Adam, God gave me my rib back. Ann isn't perfect, but she is absolutely perfect for me.

Willie

Second Chances

We all have big changes in our lives that are more or less a second chance.

Harrison Ford

Before meeting Willie, I had lived a very *seasoned* life: experienced, tested, and weathered. I had been married (and divorced) twice, raised two amazing sons, worked for a wonderful company, authored one book, and traveled to various locations preaching and inspiring others.

Yep, I encountered challenging times, suffered setbacks, disappointments, and what felt like failures. I made some stupid decisions that should have radically changed my life or ended it. I faced moments of spiritual and emotional rebellion. Yet, God spared life, and I am still alive to talk about it. And I have learned over the years that we can either drown in regret, or we can learn from the mistakes and thrive in the lessons.

Forget second chances! For God gave me *numerous* opportunities to get my act together. And, perhaps more importantly, He never gave up on me, even when I felt like giving up on myself.

In the nutshell, my life has been full of *grace*, which is "God giving me what I don't deserve."

All of us *need* grace. And if we are willing to be honest, we have all done or said something that hurt others. We've all disappointed someone. However, when we are terribly sorry for what we have done, it's important to receive God's grace so we can move forward.

I learned a lot about these things while ministering in jails and prisons for years. In getting to know men and women who were serving sentences from two to twenty years, I really got an up close and personal view of what God's grace looked like. I got a good look at people whom, while they may not have believed they deserved another chance, God's grace covered in spite of themselves and despite what they had done. And I realized grace is also God's empowerment to do the things we cannot do for ourselves.

Honestly, I could cry when I think about the grace these men and women needed to forgive themselves, believe their lives still have meaning, and keep waking up each day and giving God thanks. I recognize that grace because it is the exact same thing I was given to survive abusive relationships, start a new life after divorce, and forgive myself for having an abortion as a teenager. Grace!

Some people may wonder why I spend so much time trying to help those who are incarcerated. "If they did the crime," some might say, "they should do the time." And that is true. However, during that time, *many* change. Many heal. Many mature. Especially if they were arrested as a teenager.

And once they serve their time in prison, that punishment should not follow them into their release. Yet, many "returning citizens" must overcome the continued and constant judgment and criticism of a past that God redeemed.

Can you remember a time when you did something you deeply regretted? You asked for forgiveness, and the person said they forgave you. But every chance they got; they threw it back in your face? That did not feel good, did it? Can you imagine if God did that to us? Geesh!

A large percentage of men and women who are incarcerated are eventually released. What does that mean? It means that one day, after serving their time, they will head back to their communities. Our communities. They will shop alongside us in Walmart. They will worship with us in church. They will bring their sons or daughters to sporting events and recitals. And, yes, as is my case, they may even become our families.

After being in prison for years, they do not need to feel imprisoned *again* by those who lack grace. Any individual who has made the conscious effort to become a better person deserves the opportunity to live their best life, the opportunity to atone for past mistakes.

These are just a few things I learned from being involved with prison ministry and it tenderized my heart with the grace needed to realize God had sent Willie to me. If I had lacked the grace and discernment when I met him, I would have missed what God had for me. So, I am grateful for the grace (empowerment) needed to see who God had created him to be, not the mistake made when he was 17 years old.

My prayer for you today is that you would accept the grace God has for you. Accept that you made a mistake, but know you are *not a mistake.* Know that there is power for you to recover from whatever tried to take you out. Know that you can have a second chance if you genuinely want one. When we can accept God's grace, we can freely give it to others.

> *"I could have been dead, sleeping in my grave. But GOD blessed me to see another day. Even when I did wrong, He was still there. I'm so glad that God still hears a sinner's prayer."*
>
> *A Sinner's Prayer by Deitrick Haddon*

The words to the above song are so powerful! More importantly, they are so relevant to my life, my testimony. For I truly could have been dead and gone, so many ways, so many times. Except for the grace and mercy of the Most High God.

By now you know that I was incarcerated, but I was actually arrested and charged with two counts of Malice Murder. Even though I was 17 years old and had never been in any kind of trouble before, the authorities sought the death penalty, not because of the crime (which I confess was stupid and senseless);

but because they were frustrated that I would not cooperate with them.

You see, they wanted me to falsely implicate a good friend of mine, someone they considered a *bigger fish*. They wanted me to say he "ordered me to assassinate" a business rival; and because I refused to do so, they took it personally and became determined to destroy me, to see me fry in the electric chair. And I probably would have died a horrific death if something miraculous had not happened.

Believe it or not, one of the mothers of the two young men who tragically lost their lives expressed *sympathy* for me and my family. Who does that? Even though she was grieving the loss of her son's life, I believe God gave her the eyes to see that we were all caught up in the toxic cycle of selling the drugs placed in African American communities to facilitate our mutually assured destruction. That is, we all were victims. There would be no winners, only losers. There would be no real justice and frying me in the electric chair would not bring her precious son back.

Whatever her reason, this woman's expression of sympathy broke me. For the first time in my life, I came face-to-face with a loving and merciful God. I was not saved at the time, but I knew beyond a shadow of a doubt that it was the grace of God being poured out over my life.

Therefore, even though the judge sentenced me to serve two consecutive life sentences, I believed God was giving me a new lease on life... Life instead of death. I was being given a second chance, a new beginning, and I was determined to do everything within my power to make the best of it, even though I was going to prison – I was still alive! I wanted to live, and I wanted to do something positive and productive with my life.

Listen, when I tell you the grace of God is real, I mean it! When I tell you that He spared my life so I could get to know Him and come to understand my purpose, I am not just talking - I could have been dead and gone and sleeping in a grave, but God blessed me to see another day! And He did not stop there.

You see, while serving time in some of the worst prisons in Georgia, God kept me. His protection and favor surrounded me. His grace gave me the power to ask for forgiveness from everyone I hurt and disappointed. His grace gave me the power to forgive those who hurt me and my family. His grace gave me the power to forgive myself. His grace gave me the opportunity to take advantage of every program offered to me in prison, to accomplish things other people could not. Glory be to God, His grace opened the doors of prison, after nearly thirty-one years, and allowed me to go home healthy, whole, and in my right frame of mind, a better man.

How could I not believe in second chances when I am living it? By the grace of God, I never forget where I was for all those years. I will never forget what I have seen Him do.

It is *our* prayer that if you are fortunate enough to have been given a second, third, or fourth chance, you will choose to make the absolute best of it.

Blessings are often wrapped in adversity and strength often manifests itself at the point we feel our absolute weakest.

Do not dwell in the past. Stop looking over your shoulder. It is time to move forward and live!

With God, all things are possible (Mark 10:27).

Our Amazing Moms

They instantly became the best of friends. When we hang out together, they cling to each other like long, lost sisters who had been reunited. Both are little in size, but big in stature.

Praying Mommas

I absolutely adore and highly respect Willie's mom, Priscilla. As it happened, I had the pleasure of meeting her before I met him, and I quickly realized she is one of the strongest women I know. Faithful and big-hearted, she is full of wisdom, and a joy to be around.

When Willie and I first communicated, I was still living in Florida and had to travel to Georgia to meet him in person for the first time. When I arrived there, his precious mom allowed me to stay in her home; and I could not believe how hospitable, loving, and supportive she was of our relationship. After all, I was practically a stranger.

But not for long. As I really *connected* with her and got to know her over the weekend, I learned she drew strength from God and trusted Him to take care of her son. More importantly, she knew God was in control, and her confidence in Him inspired me. I was also encouraged by the way this beautiful woman had stood behind and stood with her son all throughout the years. She never gave up on him, never left his side, visiting him, supporting him, and always *praying* for him.

If I had not met her, I would have missed the significance of Willie giving me the highest compliment he could give a woman when he told me that I reminded him of his mom. He said this *before* I met her, so when I did, I was honored. Especially since his respect, admiration, and love for his mom was so obvious and deserving – please do not get me wrong and think Willie is a "Mama's Boy," because he is the opposite, not the type to place anyone on a pedestal; however, he is not beyond giving his mom her props.

That said, I proudly *received* this great compliment because I, too, have sons. I, too, have stood with them over the years through their ups and downs. And even though I could try to take the credit for my allegiance to them, I must give the credit where it is due – to God!

I have done my best to be available for my sons, but I am positive my prayers were with them in locations I personally could not be. My prayers were with them in situations I was not aware of. My prayers were with them in dark times as a light, covering them, and I am certain that is why they were not strung-out on drugs, in prison, or in the grave before their 21st birthdays, as with too many young men of color.

The prayers of a momma are powerful and effective! Never underestimate them. And never undervalue them.

Over the years, I have come to appreciate and even expect my mom, Janet, to pray for me. In fact, I cannot help but smile at the thought of my beautiful mom becoming a woman of prayer because, growing up, we were not exactly that praying family who attended church. Nevertheless, after my mom and dad divorced after 27 years, she had to recreate herself and eventually discovered her true identity in the Lord.

Needless to say, I greatly admire, honor and respect my mom. Not only is she an incredible example of strength for my sister and I, but she also has a heart of gold. She loves fiercely. She will give you the shirt off her back. And she is very protective of family.

Truly, I thank God for my mom's prayers. However, this is not to say that our dads do not pray. Because they do. But traditionally speaking, it is the prayers of women who selflessly and tirelessly cried out for their families, communities, and our nation that have reached God's ears, touched His heart, and moved His hand.

I am still evolving as a mom as I seek God's wisdom and discernment to purposefully pray for my adult sons. No matter how old our children get, what situations they find themselves in, what decisions they face, or what issues they struggle with; they will never outgrow the need for prayers.

Fortunately, between my mom and Willie's mom, I have two beautiful and shining examples of true women of God. Two praying mommas. I love them both and I honor them. Their lives were not easy, their struggles were real, but they have emerged as powerful women of faith!

My heart goes out to you if you have never had a mom that prayed for you. Perhaps your mom was not a Christian or a woman of faith. Perhaps she is not one now, still lost and confused. And maybe she is not setting the best example. Or maybe she simply is not involved with your life for whatever reason.

I have learned that a person cannot give what they do not have. Still, because you did not get what you needed from your mom, it does not mean you cannot get it. The cycle can be broken, and it needs to begin with you!

When we realize we did not get what we needed, it is our responsibility to get it. And then it is our responsibility to give it to others who need what we now have

Please do not be discouraged, because there is still hope for you. It is not too late for you to become better than her and do better than her. So, I implore *you* to be the person you wish your mom were. I implore you to connect with the God who created you and will never leave you nor forsake you.

Whew! I get excited about the topic of praying mommas. Believe me, if you ever want to hear me preach on any given day, all you have to do is ask me about my praying momma. Ask me why I am alive and well today. Ask me why I am a man of tremendous faith. Ask me why I believe what I believe. Ask me why I believe "beyond a shadow of a doubt" and by "the preponderance of the evidence" that God is real and there's power in the name of Jesus.

Well, let me tell you, it all began with a mother who prayed for me. A desperate momma.

As you can imagine, when I was arrested my momma probably felt like she had been sacked by a 300-hundred-pound linebacker. Blindsided. After all, she raised me better than that, and she had no idea about the mess my brother and I had gotten involved with – a mess that had started as a snowball and morphed into a snow monster.

Nevertheless, much to my mom's credit, as my little world was imploding, as the girl who had promised to love me forever was jumping ship at the first sight of the iceberg, as my best friend was stabbing me in the back, and as the media was painting an ugly picture of me, my momma weaved the mess and drew closer to me instead of running away. Even though she had to be embarrassed, disappointed, and hurt, she never expressed it. She never made it about her. And she never judged me or condemned me.

No, her youngest of three children was in deep trouble, and she was determined to be there for me. Unfortunately, she did not know anything about the law, and she couldn't afford to hire a high-profile attorney – she did retain a lawyer from her church, but it became apparent he couldn't save me from the water I was drowning in.

At that point, there was only one thing she could do... pray... pray... and keep on praying.

Aside from her prayers, my momma attempted to introduce me to a Wonderful Counselor, an

Advocate for our every need. But truth be told, I was not trying to hear anything about the "white man's" Jesus. I was not trying to hear anything about religion. And I politely asked her to stop sending all that spiritual nonsense *every day* in the mail, but she ignored me. So, I asked not so nicely. Still, she ignored me and continued to send everything I needed to know about accepting Jesus Christ as my Lord and Savior.

In hindsight, I thank God my momma did not give up and continued to plant seeds of faith in my heart. And I thank God she continued to pray for me. Now, mind you, my momma has never been the one to say those long and elaborate prayers. Never been the one to speak in tongues. Never been the one to lay prostrate on the floor for hours. No, that has never been her.

While I can appreciate those who do all that, if they are operating in the gifts of the Holy Spirit, my momma touches me with her simple yet powerful prayer: "Lord, have mercy!"

If the situation seems to be overwhelming, she may say: "Fix it, Jesus." Or she may just moan, "Jesus, Jesus, Jesus."

Fondly, I remember an in-depth conversation I was having with her one day about the injustices of the world, the unconstitutionality in the courtroom, the arbitrary and capricious denial of parole, the disproportionate number of African American men in prison, etc. I was on a role when she stopped me with these words: "Willie, I don't know about all that. But one thing I do know, God is still in control."

Man, I *felt* those words. Like she had literally placed her hand through my chest to deposit those words deep into my heart. Deep into my spirit. And let me tell, no truer words have ever been spoken! God is and always will be in control.

He was certainly in control when He brought Ann into my life, and it was confirmed that she would become my wife when my momma took an instant liking to her. No kidding, after spending time with her, my momma was like: "Thank God for Ann!" And that meant more to me than I ever thought it would because, in the past, I have never cared if my parents or my siblings liked the person I chose to date.

But it was different with Ann because I was mature, wiser, and spiritually discerning. And after spending so much time in prison, the last thing I wanted was a whole bunch of unnecessary drama in my life. The last thing I needed was for my family to have beef with my wife, and God knew that.

To be fair, my momma is a sweet lady who rarely dislikes anyone. Yet, her connection with Ann was off the charts, as if Ann were her long, lost daughter finally coming home. Or perhaps Ann was simply the wife my momma had prayed for me to have.

Whatever it was, it was eye-opening for me, as it occurred to me how much Ann and my momma were alike. Interesting really, in addition to the five billion things Ann and I had in common, it was like my momma had raised her. Not just because they both were amazing mothers. No, it was more than that.

When I say that Ann reminded me of my momma, it was because their core values were identical: *honest* and *dependable*. Acquiring it from my mom, I seriously believe that you should "say what you mean and do what you say." For that is what my momma modeled for years, and I had never met anyone on her level, until Ann.

But wait, there is more! Another confirmation for me that Ann would become my wife was when I met her momma, Janet. Another instant connection. From day one, she saw *me*, not what other people may have thought about me, not even entertaining the worst thoughts some mothers may have about their daughter becoming involved with someone in prison. Yes, she saw right into my soul, and she knew that I would be great for her daughter. And she immediately loved me and supported us, as if I were her own son.

As if that was not enough, when our mothers met, it was difficult to ignore that God was doing something *extraordinary* here. Heck, even "Blind Mellie Jelly" could see it. And talk about a beautiful picture! Remarkably and amazingly, these two women, both standing about five feet on a good day, embraced each other as if they were long, lost sisters. Thinking about it makes me speechless, witnessing how well they get along, unconsciously holding hands sometimes and all that. So touching.

Wrapping it up, let me tell you about Janet's husband, Les. He is a wonderful man of God who appreciates his wife and treats her well, the kind of husband both Ann and her momma prayed that Ann would one day have. Well, even though we do not deeply delve into the zodiac stuff, Les and I are both Aries, as our birthdays are one day apart. And yes, you may have guessed it, we are so much alike, especially the affectionate way we honor and cherish and love our wives.

Similarly, my father adores Ann and treats her like his own daughter. More importantly, he acknowledges her calling and deeply respects her gifts, recognizing that she is a tremendous woman of faith and the best thing to happen to me.

I'm telling you, only God could write this story. And I wish I could describe what it is like when our parents get together. To say that our parents have become the best of friends is an understatement, as it should be since we are *family*.

Having fun and enjoying life, one of the things we love to do (besides eat my mom's delicious cooking!) when we are all together is have a jam session at my dad's home, in his man cave full of musical instruments. Talk about making a joyful noise!

My heart overflows with joy as I realize all of this happened because of prayers and a faithful God Who heard them and answered them. While we spoke a lot about praying moms, we cannot leave out the dads who also pray for us. Between my dad, Ann's dad, and stepdad, we are covered in prayer daily! And we thank God for them as well.

It is our prayer that if you are a parent who has been praying for a son/daughter but feel like your prayers are not being answered, keep praying... praying... and keep on praying. Keep believing that God hears, and He will answer in His impeccable timing and in His perfect way. Remember that God's ways are not like ours (Isaiah 55:8), so do not miss when He *does* answer your prayers differently than what you thought or hoped. He knows how to get his/her attention and what is best for your child.

God has placed a powerful purpose in your child. Align your prayers with His Word, speak His promises over them, and believe that your prayers will usher your child into God's presence and place/keep them on the right path.

Whatever you do, do not ever stop praying!

Graduation Ceremony (February 2017)

Willie successfully completed his Mentorship Program. Words cannot express how proud I was to stand beside him and with him. Doesn't my smile say it all?

Ann

The Gift of Freedom

When Ann and I started getting to know each other, she marveled at how *free* I was. Yes, I was physically incarcerated, but I refused to be mentally, emotionally, and spiritually imprisoned, too. Remember, I viewed my sentence as a blessing, and I was determined to live my life with an attitude of gratitude.

What else could I do, sit around feeling sorry for myself? No, that was not an option, simply because I had made the decisions that landed me in prison. And since I did not intend to spend the rest of my life there, I made another executive decision, to *focus on freedom.* To focus on the numerous things I could do instead of lamenting on the things I could not do. To focus, more importantly, on what I would do once I was released.

It was not that difficult really, because there were a lot of positive things to keep me busy and focused. For the first few years, for instance, I was going to vocational trade school during the day and attending college in the evening. Even though I was initially incredibly young when I was incarcerated, I had just gotten my G.E.D., and that was a door-opener for me.

Receiving a great education combined with spiritual growth helped me to realize that freedom was a choice. Yet, the more I learned and the more I focused on freedom, the more I thought I could get myself out of the mess I had gotten myself in. In fact, I became convinced that I was smarter than the people who had sentenced me to serve *two* consecutive Life sentences – duh, didn't they realize that I only had *one* life?

Nevertheless, even though I aced my Business Law and Criminal Law classes in college, spent thousands of hours in the law library, filed hundreds of pleadings with every court with jurisdiction, and mailed dozens of petitions to the parole board, I reached the foregone conclusion that I apparently was not as brilliant as I thought I was. More precisely, even though the law was in my favor because countless "errors" had been made in my case, "the law couldn't set me free."

Interestingly, God gave me the spiritual insight to understand the parallel implications of Jesus coming in the flesh to do what the law could not do. You see, after God gave Moses the law (the ten commandments), the Israelites soon realized they could not obey the *entire* law. Learning about it did nothing to stop them from sinning – the law could not free them. No, it did more to highlight their shortcomings, making them feel guilty, hopeless, and imprisoned by their fleshly desires. And while they sacrificed animals to atone for their sins, it did not eradicate the *desire* to sin.

Then came Jesus! He was the atonement for their sins, and our sins, once and for all. Understand though, He was not sent to get rid of the law but to fulfill the law and help us to understand how, only through Jesus, can we experience freedom and not be slaves to sin.

Man, this was so powerful, because of what I experienced, after doing everything I could to set myself free. Well, not *everything*. There was only one thing left: try Jesus! Surrender it all to Him. Trust Him. Depend on Him. Believe in Him.

In doing so, I stopped focusing on myself and my situation – I seriously let go and let God! Instead of working to meet my own needs, I delved into serving others. More importantly, I concentrated on using my gifts and talents to be a blessing to others, to do my part to build a nation obedient to God. Working with the counseling department, teaching behavior modification classes, became one of my favorite pastime activities. At the top of the list, of-course, was writing inspirational fiction stories. And it was as I was accomplishing these things that God, in His perfect timing, introduced Ann into my life, blessing me with a help mate.

Before Ann, I was doing good things; but together, we began to do *great* things, going to another level. The more we prayed together, the more God showed me, and the more I wanted to serve Him. The more I wanted to make a positive difference in the lives of the men surrounding me.

Remember that two-year set off? Well, believe it or not, the more I got involved with the church services, the more I mentored youthful offenders, and the more I wrote about the redemptive power of God, the quicker the time went by as the Holy Spirit was doing a miraculous work in me, for me, and through me. The more I allowed Him to use me for His glory, the more doors *and* windows were opened before me. The more opportunities were presented. The more God's favor and protection covered me. The more people prayed for me and my release even though I was not asking them to - I honestly was not focusing on it.

On one occasion, I was serving refreshments and drinks at an administrative function in the multi-purpose area when something unexpected happened. Now, mind you, I was not assigned to this area, but I often ventured over to help an overwhelmed friend. No one ever asked me why I was there or told me to leave, mainly because I was always polite, professional, and quiet. Well, on this particular day, I was happily serving drinks when an executive from the parole board stopped before me and said, "Hey Mr. Benton, it's good to see you again, but what are you still doing *here*?"

I honestly did not know what to say. He was asking me why I was still in prison, when I probably should have been asking him the same question. When it was obvious I had no answer, he smiled and encouraged me to keep my head up and stay out of trouble.

With great fondness, I remember another occasion where God laid it on my heart to produce and publish *Men of Hope: Straight Talk From Lifers.* Associated with our mentoring group, accomplishing something no other group like ours had ever done, this powerful book provided a platform for others to share their experiences and advice through poems, songs, artwork, and essays. To say that it was an audacious mission would be an understatement since we did not discuss it with nor seek approval from the prison administrative staff – I didn't need permission from man to do what God told me to do!

When our lead facilitator, Chaplain Moss, saw the beautiful book, she actually cried. Thoroughly impressed and surprised, she could not believe that we had planned and accomplished something to that extent with tremendous success, without her knowledge and without her assistance.

Not long after that, she called me to her office, anointed my head with oil, and prayed mightily over me. "Mr. Benton," she told me afterwards, "your talents are too big for this place. It is time for you to go. I don't know where you are going, but you have to get out of here."

Glory be to God, she was right. A few weeks later, I was practically kicked out of prison - no kidding! After being ordered to pack my belongings in the middle of the night, I was transferred to a transitional center in Atlanta, and I left so fast I never received the paperwork documenting that I had been granted parole pending the successful completion of work release – I still have not seen the paperwork!

Just like that, in the blurred midst of anointed events, I was essentially physically free! While I will forever be grateful for everyone God used to make this happen, I will never forget what He did when I surrendered it all to Him. He did what neither I nor the law could do and set this captive free.

Ann

I will begin by saying that I truly admire and respect my husband. And I want to be like him when I grow up. Seriously!

When I met Willie, he was one of the freest individuals I had ever met – I never would have guessed he had been in prison half his life! His attitude was unbelievably positive and contagious. His spirits were always high and lifted, and he always had a song and a praise on his lips.

Too bad I could not say the same about myself as I, after spending a lot of time with him, began to realize that I was emotionally and spiritually bound.

Crazy huh?

I would get up early on Saturday and Sunday mornings to visit Willie. I'd leave my lovely apartment, drive my nice, reliable vehicle; and yet when I would get there, he'd end up encouraging me! How does *that* happen?

Well... I had never been in a relationship with anyone that matched the depth of transparency I had with Willie. And this new level of honesty forced some hidden things into the open. Things that God wanted me to deal with so I could finally heal.

I had preached about being free. I had written about it. I posted about it on social medial all the time. However, when the rubber met the road, it was more conceptual - I knew about it but was not *living* it.

In fact, at the time, I was still battling with who everyone *thought* I was, enslaved to people's opinions, addicted to people's approval. It was important to me that people agreed with and supported the choices I made. And the most recent choice I had made to relocate to Georgia was not a popular one. Even believing I had made the right choice, I was depressed and grief-stricken by the lack of support I received.

Those feelings triggered a lot of memories and feelings attached to my past. Feelings of not being good enough. Feelings of trying to measure up. Feelings of desperately wanting to be liked and accepted.

One of the most profound things said to me during this difficult time was spoken by my younger son, who was around eighteen at the time. While spending time together I was weeping and sharing my disappointment about how certain people were treating me because of my relationship with Willie.

He asked, "Do you believe this is the person God has for you."

"Yes, absolutely!" I responded emphatically.

"Well, mom, I can't really feel sorry for you. If you believe you made the right *choice*, you must live with the repercussions that come with it. I know it's not easy, but it is the decision you made."

Wow, what wisdom! He was not being mean, and he loved on me by telling it to me straight. And he was right!

I did make my choice. I was not forced or coerced. I used my free will to choose Willie. I chose us. Now, I simply needed to choose to be free. To refuse to be a prisoner of my past failed marriages and other relationships that caused me to question my self-worth, to question who God said I am, to question what He called me to do.

Sadly, we interact with (physically) free (but emotionally and spiritually bound) prisoners every day. They are walking around without physical handcuffs but dragging emotional shackles everywhere they go. Some are doing time in a painful marriage, a dysfunctional family situation, or a destructive lifestyle. And in our image-driven society, we have mastered the ability to wear masks so no one can detect what is really happening. Worse, we learn to fool ourselves, living in perpetual denial.

Nevertheless, when we develop a true relationship with God, He will not allow us to remain self-deceived. He will give us the eyes to see and the ears to hear. He will present situations that will expose broken areas in our lives so we can look to Him to help us become healed and whole. Interestingly, He often uses relationships to accomplish this. That is why we cannot stress enough the importance of seeking God about whom you deeply connect yourself with.

The right relationships will help usher in your healing. Whereas, the wrong relationships will help to keep you broken.

There is no doubt Willie was a Godsend. When he and I began having those tough conversations, I used to sit in the visitation room with tears rolling down my eyes. I did not like it. There was nothing private about our set up. Others were sitting close by and my pride wanted to avoid those vulnerable moments. But I had to make a choice. Did I genuinely want to be free? Or did I want this relationship to be just like all the others?

I wanted freedom. I wanted honesty and transparency. And I wanted God's best for me.

Thinking back, it was *crazy* how our conversations would go. Even though Willie possessed the ability to cross examine like the best lawyers in the world, he would never pressure me or grill me with questions - that was more me, lol. But in the midst of me asking questions and trying to deflect, the Holy Spirit would have him say something or ask a question that required me to address a past issue. An issue I moved on but never healed from. Really, it was amazing how our conversations would shine a light on where I was bound. And it was incredible how therapeutic our interactions were, allowing me to express myself, release past hurts and disappointments, and grow.

The more I got to know my husband through our enlightening conversations, the more I experienced God's true love. A love that wanted me to be set free. A love that was allowing me to *choose*.

For that is exactly what Willie did daily, leading by example. He chose to walk freely in the joy and the peace of the Lord, instead of allowing his circumstances to pull him down or defeat him. He chose to live, learn, love, and grow as if he were free, believing that he would walk out of that place one day.

And until that fateful day came, Willie became determined to serve, without ever griping or complaining, something I had to learn. For the more it became obvious I had a great man of God in my life, the more I wanted him *home* with me. The more anxious and excited I became. The more I kept my eye on the calendar, counting down until the next parole review.

Nevertheless, Willie encouraged me to take my eyes off *him* and his situation to focus on the bigger picture, to focus on what God was doing. To focus on *why* He had brought us together. To trust in and believe in the wonderful plan He had for us – to believe that God was far from done with us!

Taking heed to his advice, I shifted my focus and began doing the things I had been called and positioned to do. When I met Willie, for instance, I only had one book to my credit (published four years prior); and with his assistance, I would write and publish *several* books, develop and facilitate life-changing workshops, become more involved with prison ministry in Georgia, and speak before audiences all over the country.

In doing those wonderful and fulfilling things for the Kingdom of God, I cannot tell you where the time went. I cannot tell you the last time I had even looked at the calendar when Willie called to tell me that he had been transferred to the Atlanta Transitional Center. Free at last. Free at last! My husband was finally coming home.

God has an incredible sense of humor and an uncanny way of showing His love and power. He used my physically incarcerated husband to point me toward my emotional and spiritual freedom. Freedom was no longer conceptual, but actual. And I began to live it instead of just talking about it.

It is our prayer that in reading this chapter God will reveal to your heart how blessed you are to have the gift of freedom. It is a gift. It cannot be earned. It can only be received and exercised.

We held the key to each other's freedom. God brought us together to help the other get free from our incarcerated states. We thank God because today, we are both free. Hallelujah! We are free to live the life God set out before us and we are free from having to consult others for what God approved.

You can be free too, but you must choose it. Choose to be free from regret, unforgiveness, resentment, offense, rejection, fear, worry, abandonment, and self-doubt.

We encourage you to use your gift of freedom instead of being incarcerated by whatever is keeping you from moving forward. Refuse to be limited by what others think or say and be liberated by *who* Jesus says you are. For when Jesus sets us free, we are free indeed (John 8:32).

Suddenly

In 2016, Ann wrote “Believing for Suddenly” on a sticky note and placed it on the bathroom mirror as a reminder to exercise foolish faith for my unexpected/expected release. In November 2018, I had the honor to *personally* remove the sticker as we both praised God.

Willie

Transitioning

Transition: Movement or development from one stage to another.

Merriam Webster

For the longest I envisioned what my transition from prison to home would be like. I used to dream about the awesome job I would have and the best way to convert space at my mom's house into my little bachelor spot, happily helping her with all the home improvement projects we had discussed over the years.

And I was so enthusiastic because, even though I would be a grown man living with my momma, it would be better than living in a bathroom-size cell with a man I did not really know. Wasn't anything better than that?

Having it all figured out, I did not expect the transition to be difficult. Even when someone close to me shared her concern that I was going to be "traumatized" by all that had changed in thirty years, I immediately perished that ridiculous thought. I mean, the way I saw it, while some things had indeed changed, the fundamentals of life remained the same. Sure, we now had cell phones and cars with push start buttons – heck, some cars were parallel parking for you – but none of that would be *traumatizing* for me.

Lest I seem arrogant or overconfident, may I remind you that I was not just sitting idle in prison hoping for this time to come. No, sir! From the first day that I was incarcerated I had been *planning* for this glorious day. More accurately, focusing on freedom, I had been *preparing* for this moment. That's why I obtained certifications as an electrician, electronic technician, carpenter, cabinetmaker, career guidance technician, and customer service & computer technician, staying on top of technological advancements and other things.

Yes indeed, that's why I completed over three and half years of college before the elimination of federal funding doomed the program. That's why I successfully completed all available behavior modification programs and loved to teach the Re-Entry Skills Building class.

Glory be to God, I do not have any of the horror stories associated with prison because His favor and protection covered me. His wisdom and discernment led me, and I can honestly say that my incarceration has been a blessing to me and to others, preparing for the day of my release.

All that said, while I was acutely aware that some things had indeed changed, the fact that I needed to have a job and pay my bills on time had not changed. The fact that I needed to know and obey the laws had not changed. That fact that I needed to surround myself with positive and productive people if I wanted to do positive and productive things had not changed.

Much to my dismay, in fact, when I arrived back in the city, at the transitional center; I immediately realized the more things had changed, the more things had also remained the same.

Drug and alcohol abuse, for example, was *still* prevalent. And I was intrigued by the image of guys *still* hanging out in front of the liquor stores or slanging drugs on the corners – had they really been there for thirty years, as if chained there? Didn't they realize that it was only a matter of time before they were arrested and sent to prison for an awfully long time, if they were not shot down in the streets because of the poison they pedaled?

Similarly, I could not believe the amount of people *still using* drugs. Didn't everyone know by now that drug and alcohol abuse was nothing but a sure-fire path to pain, death, and destruction? A snowball effect that nothing good could ever come from.

Lord have mercy, even a lot of the residents at the transitional center were still drinking and doing drugs, as if they didn't realize how difficult it was for most inmates to get there – less than one percent of Georgia's prison population flows through the Atlanta Transitional Center, and I knew some Lifers who'd bite their arm off for the wonderful opportunity to be there, to do the right thing.

True story, I was watching the Macon news one day when they covered a piece about a resident at the Atlanta Transitional Center who absconded because he was so high on drugs that he refused to go back to the center. Shaking my head in disbelief, like the twenty other Lifers in my dorm, I vowed not be as foolish and unappreciative as that guy when I got my chance, my once-in-lifetime opportunity.

Can you see where I am going with this? Yes, I was transferred to the Atlanta TC the next day. And yes, I was assigned to that guy's bed. No kidding! I could not make this stuff up if I tried.

Now, despite all the madness, I was certain a lot of good things had happened since I'd been gone, but they were overshadowed by the same temptations I experienced as a teenager. And as a man, I was determined not to get caught up in the same negative and destructive patterns that were plaguing our society and destroying so many lives. After being in prison for so long, I was determined to be an asset to my family and my community. And, no, I was not going back to prison! Failing was not an option. Drinking alcohol or doing drugs was not an option.

Thinking about these things, I was reminded of how blessed I was to have Ann, and how amazing God was. For with her, everything *changed.* Having relocated to Georgia from Florida, she had created a beautiful home for us, away from the city, in a new environment for both of us, and I could not wait to enjoy it.

But first things first, I needed to get a job and successfully complete the program. Fortunately, the employment coordinator at the center hooked me up with a job at a construction company. Unfortunately, it was a back-breaking assignment, as I quickly realized that I was not seventeen anymore. Yet, I did it, reminding myself that I was not going back to prison.

I also had to acknowledge one major adjustment I needed to make: I had to *speed* up to catch up and keep up with society, literally. What do I mean? Well, imagine *walking* in a single-file line for years, then one day being thrown into the fray of a busy and unruly city. Believe me, that is a sensory deprivation and thought overload process to adjust to, the kind of thing you do not think about until you experience it.

Truly, I was fascinated by and leery of the racing traffic – why was everyone in such a rush? I wondered one day as I chilled in a McDonald's and watched in bewilderment as the cars, motorcycles, and trucks sped down the road like they were insane. And let me tell you, I was not the one to stand next to the curb at the bus stop! Especially since the vehicles were moving almost faster than I could see them.

Nevertheless, doing what I needed to do, I walked, rode the bus, and caught the train every day, without complaint, despite the unpredictable Atlanta weather. And, as part of the process, I even obtained my driver's license – can you guess how fast or slow I drive today?

Seven short months later, having completed all my classes and saved enough money, I was released from the transitional center. And I was a totally free man for the first time in over thirty years. In fact, glory be to God, I actually drove myself home in our brand-new push-starting car.

Whew! I wish I could accurately describe what I experienced when I stepped inside our home for the first time - I had seen pictures and videos, but they could not compare to the real thing. Ann was intentional about making it *our* home, not just hers. Everything from the pictures on the wall, to the design of the shower curtain, and the furniture.

Truly, I thank God for my wonderful wife, as I acknowledge more and more how easy she helped make the transition for me, for us. She encouraged me, supported me, and even pushed me to do what I needed to do, and I cannot imagine having to do it without her.

In fact, my heart goes out to all the men and women who do not have the family support God blessed me to have. The struggle is real, and it is easy to understand why so many people return to prison within a few weeks after their release. Especially if they did not go to a transitional center like I did.

Understanding more and more how the system is designed to fail, I realize how important it is to have faith in God, Someone greater than the system or ourselves. And I am so grateful that I eventually had enough sense to believe in, trust in, and depend on Jesus to be the Lord of my life. For doing so has made an incredible and indescribable difference.

Ann

Prior to Willie's release, we talked about transitioning quite a bit. But, in my mind I equated the word with *his* process and not necessarily *our* process, certainly not thinking I would be transitioning too.

Yet, there I was, transitioning from living like a single person to having my husband at home. Transitioning from having everything arranged how I wanted them to be to making allowances for how he wanted things. Transitioning from being the only one managing our finances and making those decisions to both of us having an input. Transitioning from deciding for myself what speaking engagement I would accept to considering whether my husband was okay with it. If he wanted to attend. Or not attend. And if he did not, was I okay going without him.

While it was not overly complex, it was *different* and at times required us to have a "talk." And I am sure Willie was not initially prepared for all the talks I believed we needed to have. Especially since I tended to be emotional, all in my feelings, and often repeated myself.

Of-course Willie has emotions, he just does not wear them on his sleeves like I do; and he didn't mind talking, but once the point was made, he was ready to move on. Strangely, even though I did not usually hold grudges, I did get stuck in some moods and feelings. And it would bug me when he was able to move on, watch tv and be at peace, without me.

Looking back, I confess that I made things a lot more stressful for *myself* than it had to be, until I became determined not to make my husband feel like he was back in prison. Determined not to be bossy, controlling, demanding, and inflexible. Determined not to do anything that may cause him to dread coming home at night.

As I learned my husband, I discovered our taste in TV shows, music, and social media was radically different; but I had to respect it and not be threatened or bothered by it because there was absolutely *nothing* wrong with his interests, likes or dislikes. Moreover, since he never criticized anything I liked or enjoyed, I had to allow him to discover and rediscover what he enjoyed, to be himself.

More importantly, I began to understand what it means to love unconditionally, as God loves us and encourages us to come to Him as we are. With Him, we also go through a transitioning, a life-long process called sanctification, wherein the Holy Spirit helps us conform to the image of Jesus Christ. Never condemning us but teaching us and allowing us to grow, allowing us to become whole, healed, delivered, and set free, in the Mighty Name of Jesus.

During our transitioning, Willie taught me that our differences are what make us perfect for each other. For we have "rubbed off" on each other in so many ways. Our differences, instead of having us at odds, should be enhancers, if we allow them to be. Likewise, our strength and weaknesses should complement each other, as we learn to do life together.

Willie absolutely loves our home. He works hard, but there is nothing like coming home to our recliners, his workshop in the garage, our TV with the booming bass, and (most of all) his wife who loves him unconditionally. He's so good for me!

On a scale of 1-10, I would give our transition success an 8. For the most part it was exceptionally smooth, and it seems like we have been together for twenty-five years, in a good way. The two points, however, that stopped our transition from being perfect is due to our learning curve. We needed time to learn each other and extend grace. We also needed the time to get used to sharing space, ideas, opinions, and desires to remain perfect for each other.

It is our prayer that through our sharing, you will realize that life has many transitions. As we mature, we all go from one stage to another and it is important to gravitate toward what contributes to growth and avoid what can cause stagnation. Especially in a marriage.

Married couples must do all we can to grow together instead of growing apart. In the grand scope of life, we've learned that some things are not *that* serious. Some arguments are not worth winning. And there are some preferences that are just that, preferences – they should not be deal breakers.

Most of all, we have learned how much grace and time are needed for *any* life transition. Do not try to rush the process, allow things to unfold organically, and address things as they come up. Do not sweep things under the rug. Allow the other person to express their likes/dislikes. Do not make it personal, and don't be intimidated by it. Respect differences.

Trust the process. We did and we are grateful for what we have learned about ourselves and each other. Transitions are inevitable and when done correctly will yield beautiful fruit.

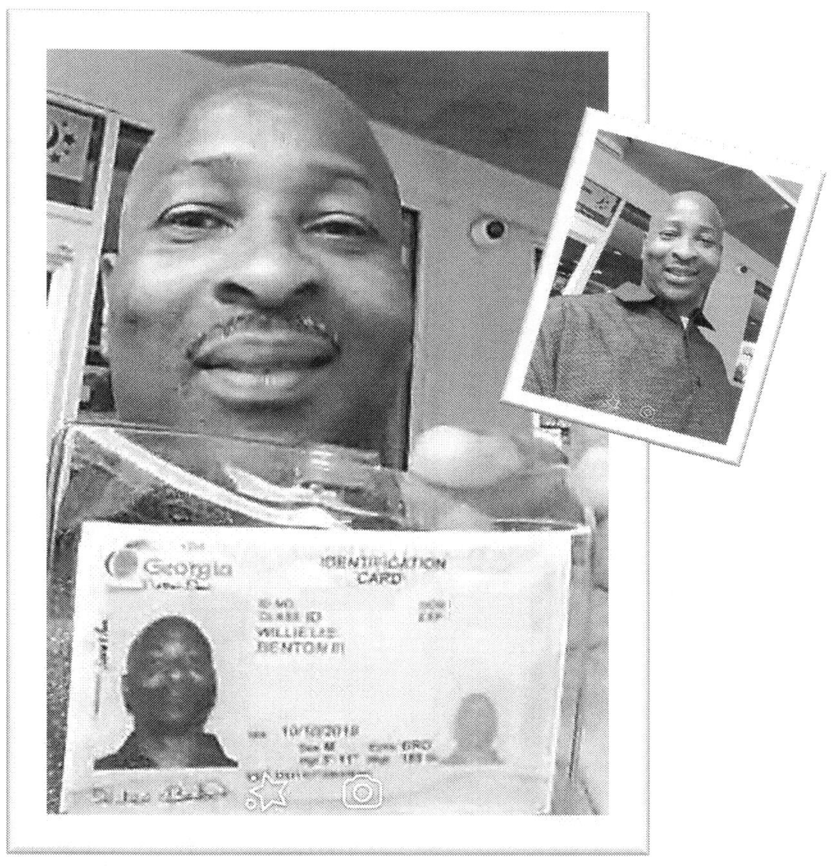

Back in Business (October 2018)

Glory be to God, it was a great day! I was back in the City (Atlanta) at the transitional center and was excited to get out and get my ID card. I was ready to work to take care of my wife and family.

Willie

True Intimacy

The antidote for loneliness is not togetherness, it's intimacy.

Anonymous

To be honest, prior to meeting Willie, the idea of intimacy was conceptual for me. I thought I knew what it meant to be intimate, but I did not have a clue. Until now. Until finally connecting with and marrying my soulmate, my best friend.

Thinking back, I remember having a conversation with a guy who attempted to convince me that husbands and wives cannot be best friends. He explained how the husband should have other friends, including female friends, if he wanted to express his feelings, etc.

Remember that famous line from Jerry McGuire: "You had me at hello?"

Well, this confused guy did not have me at all. In fact, I lost all interest when he shared his sentiments on this topic. Maybe he eventually found a wife who subscribed to that mentality, but I wanted a husband who wanted to be my absolute best friend and confidante.

While Willie and I do have close friends that we confide in and seek advice from, we never divulge anything to anyone before discussing it among ourselves first. We, in fact, never value anyone's opinion more than we value each other's.

Our understanding has led to some difficult but much needed conversations, and we have set a precedence of honesty, no matter what. Even though some have coined it "Brutal Honesty," we believe honesty does not have to be vicious. In fact, when a person's truth is spoken in love, it softens the blow a bit.

Doing anything and everything in love, as a matter of fact, is the source of true intimacy. Holding hands, sitting in the recliners next to each other while watching a really good Netflix series, feet touching in bed, washing dishes, tackling DIY projects, eating take out at our dining room table, walking in the park, listening to old school music and dancing in our bedroom, surprising each other with a bag of Neon Gummy Savers or berry flavored Skittles, forehead kisses, squeezing each other's buns as we pass by, walking under the moonlight in our backyard, a text that says: "On my way home, can't wait to see you," making a packed lunch for Willie every day, him coming home and handing me his paycheck, having disagreements, calling our parents on the weekend, being on Facetime with our granddaughter, and holding hands to pray together are all excellent examples. Big gestures wrapped in small, kind packages.

In other words, anything that draws us closer together, increases our trust, expresses love, and sets the atmosphere for transparent conversation is intimacy. Even our disagreements strengthen our bond because our truths are voiced, and our hearts are clear.

Now, because of my husband and best friend, I feel safe, valued, honored, respected, listened to, and appreciated. I feel free to be me, and I am sure all the ladies reading this right now will agree that feeling secure is the match that lights our intimacy candle.

I gave Willie my heart, and he has done nothing but protect it. That right there is the truest sense of intimacy I could ask for.

Willie

Like most men, I love and appreciate a beautiful woman. Yet, maturity, wisdom, and experience has taught me that beauty is so much deeper than skin tone and body shape. Thus, I desired an intelligent, goal-oriented, business-minded, God-fearing woman who enjoyed reading and writing. A woman who could encourage me to become the best version of myself, while always striving to become her best self.

By now you know that God outdid Himself with Ann. You know she is everything I prayed for and more. You know that we have true intimacy in our marriage. And you undoubtably know how much we love each other.

But can you imagine how much more God loves us? How much more He loves her? How much more He loves me? How much more He desires true intimacy with us? How much more He desires true intimacy with you?

If any of this seems foreign or inconceivable to you, I strongly encourage you to begin with a look back at Adam and Eve. Upon their creation and placement in the Garden, they enjoyed true intimacy with God. They enjoyed communing with Him, and He relished interacting with His greatest creation until sin (separation) entered the world because of their disobedience. In punishing them for their waywardness, God also inevitably penalized Himself because He still desired to be intimate with His masterpiece.

His desire, in fact, was so strong that He sent His only begotten Son, Jesus, to carry out the ultimate plan to reconcile us to Himself, to remove the barrier (sin) that separated us for once and for all. In doing this, Jesus enjoyed true intimacy with His disciples and everyone He encountered while walking in the flesh, teaching them, empowering them, healing, them, eating with them, forgiving them, and even washing them.

As if that was not enough, Jesus suffered a brutal and undeserving death on the cross for them. For you. For me. For *everyone* who believes in Him.

But wait, the narrative does not end there! For on the third day, Jesus arose from the grave to defeat death, to give us power over sin, to remove the barrier. Then, according to the brilliant plan, He returned unto the Father, opening heaven's door for the Holy Spirit to come and restore true intimacy with *believers*. To connect with those who have been called and chosen.

Let me be the first to tell you, it takes a *foolish faith* to believe any of this. It takes a foolish faith to believe that God is real and cares for us. It takes a foolish faith to trust in Him and depend on Him. And it really takes a foolish faith to believe there is power in the Mighty Name of Jesus!

Well, when I look in the mirror, I see the biggest fool of fools! For I took a chance and tried Jesus. Seriously, I got down on my hands and knees in a filthy one-man cell and accepted Jesus as my Lord and Savior, and He saved a sinner like me. More importantly, He sent the Holy Spirit to dwell inside of me, to have true intimacy with Him. To hear from Him. To learn from Him. To walk with Him. To obey Him. To worship Him. To praise Him. And to glorify Him.

Glory be to God, I absolutely love the wonderful wife who jumped into the fire with me, but I love Jesus so much more for dying on the cross for my sins. For healing me, restoring me, delivering me, and setting me free. For showing Himself to be real to me.

Similarly, Ann loves her adorable, encouraging, and supportive husband (me); but she loves Jesus so much more because of the amazing things He has done in her, through her, and for her. For the remarkable things He has done for her family, her closest friends, and her supporters.

While Ann and I often pray together, a powerful example of our true intimacy, we also realize how important it is to develop our *personal* relationships with Our Father. Likewise, it is equally important that we seek the face of the Lord during our personal study and devotional time because He speaks to us in various ways and at different times. Articulating this reminds me of the numerous times Jesus separated Himself from His disciples to pray privately and intimately, a divine illustration of wisdom and discernment we all should adhere to.

It is our prayer that through our sharing, you will desire to not only have intimate interactions with family and friends but also experience true intimacy with God. You see, intimacy was never meant to be for marriage only. No, it was intended for everyone and everything we hold dear to us. And we should desire to love no one and no thing more than we love God, Our Great Creator.

When we break down the word *intimacy,* it can also look like "Into Me See." It is a position of vulnerability, wherein all pretenses and defenses are let down. Dare to be real with God and watch how real He will reveal Himself to you.

Similarly, in all other deeply connected relationships, especially marriages, seek to allow others to see who you *really* are. Celebrate the good in each other and extend grace for areas where growth is needed. Unconditional love is one of the greatest platforms for true intimacy, as we love others as Jesus Christ loves us.

Our First Selfie (November 2018)

While some might view taking a selfie as “no big deal,” it was for us. This was our first time being able to take a free picture (had to pay for pictures in prison) and not have someone dictate our pose.

Complete Not Compete

For a long time, I have been confident in who I am in God. Thus, I have never been the one to actively seek approval and acceptance from others. Nor have I ever been the one to become jealous and envious of what God has equipped others to do, being thankful for the gifts and talents He placed in me. More importantly, I passionately believe what God has for me is for me.

This mindset makes me perfect for Ann. Even though she is undoubtably my soulmate, and despite the numerous things we have in common, her incredible strengths and undeniable weaknesses are different from mine.

That said, I believe the goal of a help mate is to not only help us achieve our purpose, but also to help us evolve into the man/woman God has created us to be. So, when God blesses us with a help mate, we must be open to acknowledging and appreciating the strengths they have, especially if the strengths highlight and even complement our weaknesses.

If we are not willing to acknowledge our need for assistance or improvement, we can turn our spouse into a competitor instead of an ally. Sadly, some couples can be in direct competition with each other by using their strength as a prideful way to constantly have the "one up" on the other. Or worse, a strength can be used to belittle a spouse, and that spirit of competition can cause strife, lack of flexibility, and even resentment. Neither person wants to feel inferior, and neither person wants to submit to the other.

By the way, the word *submit* is not evil, because it is not synonymous with control. No, it's more about humility and serving, and it is Biblical for both the husband *and* the wife to submit to each other, to respectfully defer to the other.

With this understanding, I appreciate Ann's respectful acknowledgement (submission) of me being the head of our home. She trusts that my *intention* is always to do what is best for her/us and to do what pleases God. But I am *not* the authority on every topic we discuss or every situation we encounter. There are several things Ann does better than me, and I yield to her authority, experience, insight, and suggestions regarding them. Similarly, if I am not exactly hearing from God on a topic, I have no problem seeking her wise counsel. The same way she allows me to bring my expertise, strengths, and insight to any given situation.

Our honesty and receptivity in this area allows us to work well together, especially since we know and embrace our strengths and weaknesses. For example, it is clear to us that while Ann is a good writer, she is a phenomenal speaker; I am often in awe of how God uses her, amazed by her ability to "free-style," speaking without notes and preparation, speaking what the Holy Spirit gives her.

While I, on the other hand, am a good speaker, we both agree that I am an exceptional writer and am more knowledgeable about writing. Thus, when we host an event, I have no problem being in the background and I am cool if I do not speak, trusting that she will represent us quite well. I can be in the audience, or I can stand next to her. In whatever way she needs my help, she has it. And I do not need to be *seen* doing it, simply because I love to support and encourage my wife.

Likewise, when it comes to our various writing projects, Ann often defers to me in some matters, like content editing for instance. She depends on me to decipher and envision exactly what our clients need to deliver their message succinctly. And she consults me for all final format and creative design issues.

In essence, since we are not competing against one another, we can allow each other to lead and trust each other enough to follow. We can allow each other to shine, without feeling the need to steal the spotlight. Without feeling threatened in some way. Without feelings of jealousy and envy. Without feeling like one person is always right while the other person is always wrong. Without treating each other like enemies instead of allies.

This is especially important because we both have a lot to contribute, in different ways, to the ministry we have been blessed to have. And it allows us to work together, on one accord, to achieve our common goals. If this were not the case, God forbid, we would not get anything done. Thus, we are extremely grateful for the Holy Spirit leading us and guiding us, keeping us humble and united.

Unfortunately, another type of competition in relationships occurs when you must compete with another person's idea of who they think you should be. For when a person connects with you based on who you *can* become instead of who you are, actively seeking to change you and improve you, that is a tractor trailer wreck in the middle of a busy highway.

As you can imagine, this is an uncomfortable and self-depreciating place to be because there's nothing worse than a person forcing you to dress, behave, speak, and think the way that person believes you should. As if you were a puppet on someone's short string. As if you were that person's science fair project. As if you were not uniquely created on purpose for a purpose.

Make no mistake about it, being deeply connected with a person who is constantly trying to change you is exhausting and debilitating. It can also be demeaning. If you are with a person who says they will love you more if you would only...this and that...your relationship is in trouble.

Not being accepted and loved for who you are (flaws and imperfections), should be a deal breaker!

Now, do not get me wrong, I'm not suggesting that we should not want our mate to reach his or her full potential, because we should. However, withholding love, honor, and respect because a person is not there yet, is emotional blackmail. And straight-up childish.

More importantly, it is unrealistic. Yet, often, it seems people fall in love with 20% of who a person is and 80% of who the person has the potential to become. This should be flipped around. Fall in love with 80% of who they are and be a cheerleader for the remaining 20%. And if, for whatever reason, the full potential is not actualized, you still win. Like buying a car because you like the current design and value instead of what it may be worth in five years.

Quite frankly, if you recall, that's exactly what I had to do with Willie. I had to decide if I still wanted to be with him if he were never released from prison, and it was an easy decision for me because I was certain he was the man God had for me, not because of the potential of achieving great things once he was released.

Similarly, Willie had to decide if he wanted to be connected to the good *and* the bad he saw in me. The *real* me. You see, in the past I had made desperate attempts to become who someone else thought I should be, only to discover that was a form of emotional and psychological imprisonment. And by the time I met Willie, I was beyond that foolishness, as I was discovering more and more of who I am, daughter of the Most High God.

Fortunately, from the first day I met him until now, Willie has only asked me for two things: One, he wants me to always be myself. Two, he wants me to "say what I mean and do what I say." In other words, he just wants me to be my *authentic* self. Always.

Today, I can honestly say I am freer than ever simply because Willie has never made me feel like I need to be smarter, thinner, more/less spiritual, or anyone other than who I am. And since there is nothing worse than being in competition with a person's concept of who they *want* you to be, I am grateful that we have embraced each other's flaws and all. Taking the good with the bad. Loving each other unconditionally. More importantly, walking in the grace and mercy of the Lord, we have learned to extend the same thing to each other.

It is our prayer you will ascertain and acknowledge whether there is a spirit of competition active in your relationship. Destroying it from within.

Do not compete. Learn to work together. And never make the other person feel like they are competing with who you *want* them to be instead of loving them for who they are.

Also, be careful of causing your spouse to feel like he/she is competing with your past. That's huge! And it is important to understand that the past is best left where it belongs, behind you.

When God connects two people to spend the rest of their lives together, they become a team, on one accord. They become allies, as well as each other's biggest cheerleader. They become helpers and healers, since the goal is to enhance and build up, not to tear down and destroy. To complete not compete. Rest assured that anything other than this is not of God and has no heavenly value.

First Home Visit (November 4, 2018)

This was a glorious day. Willie received his first 6-hour pass, allowing him to step into our apartment for the first time. It felt like he had always been there.

Ann

Forgiveness

To forgive is to set a prisoner free and discover that the prisoner was you.

Lewis B. Smedes

The topic of *forgiveness* is one that Ann and I discuss often. It is a deep and life-altering subject since forgiveness does not come natural to most of us. Yet, if not done regularly, it can and will be a great hindrance to our well-being. That is, it can and will eat us alive from the inside out. Believe me, I have fought that vicious battle, and I still have the scars to prove it.

Unforgiveness steals, kills, and destroys. It steals our peace, kills our joy, and destroys our blessings!

By now you know that I was in prison for over thirty years for an awful and senseless crime I committed when I was seventeen. But get this, I did not just wake up one day and decide to shoot two people for no reason. No, it started with a previous (seemingly harmlessly) decision to sell drugs with my brother and a group of guys looking to expand their illegal operation from Miami to Georgia.

Not long after I connected with this lucrative venture, my brother, without my consent or my knowledge, *stole* some guns and drugs from them, intending to go into business with a shady woman he just met.

Wait, it gets worse. My brother did not tell me what he'd done! So, in my ignorance, I hooked up with these guys the next day as usual, only to be snatched up, beaten, and questioned about what my brother had done.

Can you imagine being hit upside the head with an Uzi, or having a nickel-plated .44 magnum shoved down your throat, while being interrogated about something you know absolutely nothing about? Something you had absolutely nothing to do with! No words can describe the range of emotions coursing through my body, or the evil thoughts racing through my mind.

Then the unthinkable happened. The phone rung, and these guys learned that my unsuspecting brother was around the corner. Being optimistic, as I was being dragged to the car, I was thinking that after we *talked* about it, we'd all be laughing at the mistake later, after I calmed down and maybe hit a couple of them back.

Silly me! When these guys rolled up on my brother's car, there was no discussion. No verbal warning. No, when they saw him, they swiftly emerged from their cars and opened fire, shooting like we were in the wild, wild West. And as I stood there, stunned, watching in slow motion as the slugs riddled my brother's car, breaking glass, puncturing metal, deflating tires, I saw my brother go down.

I watched him fall! And I just knew he was dead. Shot down in the mean streets of Atlanta. Right before my eyes. While I could do nothing. Nothing!

Everything changed in that moment. Everything naïve, innocent, and harmless within me disappeared. And while I do not remember how I got away; I did manage to escape unharmed. Unharmed yet damaged. Yes, I got away, but I was still there, forever changed by the incident.

Similarly, my dear brother limped away with his life but with a bullet wound to his leg, only by the grace of God. And when I saw him in the hospital, after having to tell our mother he was there, I knew our lives would never be the same. I also knew those responsible would pay for what they did to him, for what they did to me, and for threatening my *family*. Threatening to harm my precious baby boy if we went to the authorities about the incident.

However, going to the police was the last thing on my mind. No, I was too upset, frightened, and thirsty for revenge. I could not eat, sleep well, or forget, as I was literally being eaten alive from the inside. And I thought the only way to overcome what I was feeling was to take the law into my own hands.

But I was wrong about that. Taking matters into my own hands did not make me feel better or solve anything. And being arrested for two counts of Malice Murder only made things worse. For me. For my family. For those guys' family. For our community.

Still, honestly speaking, for years I believed I did the right thing. Given the same circumstances, I strongly believed I would do the same thing. And even though I had experienced the power of forgiveness (and God's grace) through the mother who expressed sympathy for me and my family, it was still a foreign concept to me.

Until I met Ann. If you recall, I was coming up for parole for the fifth time shortly afterwards and I remember sharing my disdain for the inevitable parole interview wherein I would be asked about the crime. Questioned about something that had happened twenty-five plus years ago. Questioned about something I wanted to be done with, especially since it always seemed like I was attempting to rationalize or justify what I had done, when in fact it was what it was. At that point, I had done the crime, and I had done the time. So, I was ready to go home. Period.

As it happened, around that time, Ann's oldest son drove to Georgia from Florida to personally meet me, the man his mother was planning to marry, to judge for himself – God bless him!

In talking to him, face to face, I explained what happened that fateful night and how I simply made the best of a bad situation afterwards. He later expressed that he was moved by the fact I was not playing the victim of the system role and was accepting full responsibility.

Yet, as I focused on serving others and pleasing God, He showed me something different – Lord help me explain this! This was so *powerful.*

Get this, He revealed that I had not been serving time like a respectable man holding myself accountable all those years because I was accepting full responsibility for my actions. But rather, I had been operating under the power of *unforgiveness*. Think about that! For years, I had been motivated to do what I'd been doing by the rage and pain I still harbored from what I endured and witnessed that night, as well as the tremendous fallout from it. The rage and anger I did not know how to release the right way.

As Ann would explain it, I had developed an unhealthy soul tie because of what happened to me. In hindsight, it may seem like common sense to realize that I had been traumatized by it all, and this was evident by the emotions triggered when watching movies where the brother or a close family member was shot. No matter how many times I saw the same movie, I always felt some type of way, and my eyes always watered up.

Do not let the fact that I was doing positive and productive things fool you, because it does not mean I was driven by the right reason. With that in mind, have you ever been told by someone close to you that you would never do anything good with your life for whatever reason, yet you accomplished great things to prove them wrong? If so, you can understand where I'm coming from. You can understand that motivation come in all shapes and sizes, good and bad.

Glory be to God, let me tell you, the Holy Spirit was taking me somewhere, revealing that I needed to forgive to heal. To forgive others, and there were a lot of people to forgive. To forgive myself for all the disappointments and regrets I kept tucked away.

Coming to terms with all this, I recognized that I did not have to, and I should not have done what I did. Despite what happened to me and my brother, I could have done something different. I could have gone to the police, or I could have chosen to forgive them. Either way, the fact that they drew first blood was not a reason kill, harm, or maim anyone. And as the old saying goes, two wrongs do not make anything right. No, it only made me wronger.

In the same vein, I recognized that while I can never control what anyone else does, I *can* control what I do or do not do. And therein is the real meaning of being a free and responsible man with honor and integrity, doing the right thing no matter what, doing what is right no matter the cost.

Moreover, being a man of God, a Christian, is not necessarily about becoming perfect in and of myself, but about walking in a higher power to do the difficult and unnatural things. Like forgiving others. Like turning the other cheek. Like blessing those who curse you. Like having compassion for others. Like loving your neighbor as you love yourself. All the things Jesus modeled as He dwelled among us.

Taking what was revealed to heart, I acknowledged that I had been wrong and repented. I asked for forgiveness. More importantly, for the first time ever, I truly forgave others for all past offenses, big and small, breaking all unhealthy soul ties and releasing what I had unknowingly allowed to imprison me for years. And, yes, I forgave myself for all the pain and suffering I caused. For disappointing myself, my family, and my community.

Real talk, I am telling you, it was as I was serving others and pleasing God *and* learning these invaluable-long-time-coming lessons that the doors of the physical prison were finally opened. Today, I am totally free in every way, and I hope this encourages someone.

If you have done some terrible things, know that you can be forgiven. Know that you can be redeemed. Know that your life is not over. Know that your life still has a purpose, and God can still use you despite your past. Despite your mistakes. Despite your imperfections.

But you must completely *own* what you did, instead of blaming others, rationalizing, or justifying what you did. You must repent and ask God for forgiveness. You must forgive yourself. Own it, and watch God do something miraculous in you and your situation.

Believe me, if God did it for me, He can certainly do it for you!

Ann

I did not realize I was dealing with unforgiveness. Yet, sadly, I had imprisoned myself to past things I was *still* ashamed of or disappointed about. Things I did not consciously think about, even though I had neither found closure nor properly healed from them. Things that, if I continued to unwittingly hold myself hostage to them, could cause me to miss what God was presently doing.

Talking to Willie helped bring a lot of hidden things to the forefront and gave me the courage to deal with them, as he regularly reminded me of who I was in the Lord and complimented me on being a great mother. Willie also regularly encouraged me to walk boldly in the anointing God had placed in me, and I am incredibly thankful for how the Lord used him – to free me from the past so I (we) could enjoy the amazing future He has for us.

Forgiving *myself* was the first step. Then I had to forgive others. This was harder for me, honestly, because I often placed unrealistic expectations on others and became disappointed when they could not meet them. Disappointed, in fact, because they simply cannot be God or provide what only He can give me.

Notably, it is said that refusing to forgive someone is equivalent to drinking a cup of poison and expecting the person who hurt you to die. Stop and think about it! Does the concept of hurting others by hurting ourselves make sense? Of course not, because unforgiveness is not a matter of the head, it is a matter of the heart.

In other words, refusing to forgive is a *heart* issue. A broken heart issue. A disappointed heart issue. An abused heart issue. A betrayed heart issue. An unhealthy heart issue. For when we do not deal with heartbreak, we take our broken heart into other relationships, expecting someone who didn't break it to heal it. Unfairly expecting someone else to do the impossible, setting them up to fail.

When we don't forgive someone who hurt us, we end up bleeding all over ones who didn't cut us.

Anonymous

The challenge with not forgiving others is the unhealthy bond that forms between us and the perpetrator of the hurt. It knowingly/unknowingly ties us to the very thing we despise or the hurt we are trying to escape.

You see, we are three-part beings made of a body, soul, and spirit. Our soul consists of our mind (thoughts), will (decisions), and emotions (feelings). When we become deeply connected to people through our thoughts, decisions, and feelings, we link our soul to them. We create a bond which Willie previously referred to as a "soul tie." When our experience with others is positive and productive, we create a *healthy* soul tie.

On the other hand, when our experience with others introduces trauma, pain, devastation, or disappointment; an *unhealthy* soul tie is created. Clearly, it is essentially wise to break the unhealthy soul tie, yet unforgiveness too often fortifies it. Strengthens and intensifies it. Worse, the unhealthy connection seeps into our emotional, spiritual, or mental spheres and contaminates our well-being.

So... moving to another state is not going to free you from the ex who cheated on you... if you do not forgive. Cutting off your dad's access to your life and your children's lives will not give you the peace you are seeking... if you do not forgive.

Knowing this, Willie and I facilitate a workshop (online and in person) to help individuals understand how these ties are formed and how to break free. The majority of those who attend and need that freedom struggle with unforgiveness. Without question, unforgiveness has an *imprisoning* affect. And the prisoner is the one who needs to forgive and release.

We often struggle to forgive others based on our incorrect understanding of what it means to forgive and release someone. For example:

1. We think forgiving someone means we condone their behavior. It does not. We can forgive them yet be intentional about not subjecting ourselves to their careless, reckless, or selfish behavior. This may mean ending the relationship, not staying in it.
2. We think forgiving a person means we must be close to them. Forgiveness does *not* automatically mean the relationship is fixed or restored. There are some relationships (i.e., family) that we cannot cut off or end. However, we can forgive them and love them from a distance.
3. We think forgiveness is an act of weakness. We do not want to be considered a doormat they can walk all over. When a person continues to show signs of being dangerous, unhealthy, or untrustworthy, put up boundaries. Decide what you will *not* put up with and stick to it. Boundaries are not to

control others; it is to manage ourselves. Forgiveness is a strength, not a weakness.

4. We think forgiveness means forgetting what happened. It is not possible to forget. There are things and experiences in life that we cannot unfeel, unsee, unthink or unremember.

   Forgiveness does not remove the painful experience, but it does remove the sting of it. Forgiveness helps us to remember the painful event, without the pain.

5. We think forgiveness is about the other person. Wrong. There are times when the other person does not think they need to be forgiven or even cares to be forgiven. The other person may be deceased or no longer a part of our lives. In any of these instances, the other person cannot or will not initiate forgiveness. However, you cannot wait on them and you do not need their participation to release them.

Similarly, we often struggle with forgiveness because we misunderstand the negative consequences associated with unforgiveness. Here are a few *truths* about unforgiveness:

A. Unforgiveness places a wedge between us and God. We are deceived if we *think* we can have a healthy and transparent relationship with God, while refusing to do what He says. God instructs us to forgive others, and if we do not; He will not forgive us (Matthew 6:15). Powerful and gut-wrenching words.

But think about it. God sent His ONLY Son, Jesus to die for our sins, which is the ultimate demonstration of forgiveness. And our life, as a Christian, is to become more like Jesus.

Well, Jesus forgave – He even forgave Judas. So, make no mistake, it is impossible to have a healthy and genuine relationship with God while withholding forgiveness.

B. Unforgiveness is like a cancer. If not dealt with, it spreads into all aspects of our lives. It affects our relationships and ruins our testimony. If you have children, your hard heart sets a bad example, which can cause them to grow up struggling to forgive.

C. Unforgiveness hinders your blessings. God commands that we forgive others. And when we obey God's commands, He blesses us (Luke 11:28). Likewise, we cannot disregard what God says and expect Him to bless our lives (homes, families, jobs, businesses, ministry, etc.).

So, let me be very honest as I wrap up this chapter. My struggle to forgive certain individuals was *all about me* and not them. It was about my feelings of betrayal. I felt let down. I felt used. I felt taken advantage of. I felt like I suffered; and as a result, I wanted them to suffer too. I wanted them to feel my dissatisfaction. Feel my pain.

Here is the thing though, I have learned that when we make it about ourselves, we can easily declare ourselves victims. But when we get to know who we are in the Lord, being a victim is not Kingdom vocabulary.

Understand, if God *allows* a thing, He plans on using it, for your good. Point blank. If someone left you, God will use it. If someone rejected you, God will use it. If someone did not support you, God will use it.

As tough and painful as *any* situation is, God promises to work it all together for our good and His glory (Romans 8:28). So, if God will work it together, we can release people for what they did. Their plan does not trump God's plan. Especially since He can fix it and use it.

A great example is the story of Joseph in the Bible. His brothers stripped off his favorite coat, but they could not strip him of God's favor. They put him in a pit, but they could not keep him from getting to the palace.

Moreover, despite everything Joseph endured because of the ill-feelings of his brothers and others, he eventually understood how God had allowed it. He eventually understood that what his brothers meant for evil, God made it for good, turning it around, benefitting Joseph, his family, and the Children of Israel (Genesis 50:20).

Identifying with Joseph's situation, I have learned more about God from people doing me wrong than people doing me right, because the hurt and disappointment pushed me closer to Him. Made me seek His face harder. Made me desire God's will for my life even more. And the pain and disappointment made me acutely aware of an incredible strength I did not know I possessed, in Him.

With a deep desire to be obedient to God, I made the *choice* to forgive and release several people; and I am no longer tied to them, emotionally or spiritually. Some are still around, and some are long gone. Either way, they are released, and so am I. Through forgiveness, I am no longer tied to them or the pain they caused.

It is our prayer that through our sharing, you will recognize that forgiving yourself and forgiving others is a choice. It is not a feeling.

When we read about Joseph and his brothers, Joseph was hurt. When he saw them for the first time since they betrayed and rejected him, he hurt deep inside. He probably wanted to get revenge. He was second in command, so he clearly had the power to hurt them back. But he had a greater power that came from a greater purpose. A purpose that was bigger than his brothers.

We pray that you will allow God to give you the courage and humility needed to set yourself and others free. Your future success hinges on it.

Our First Thanksgiving (November 2018)

Even though Willie was still at the transitional center, words cannot express how ecstatic we were to have him home. In previous years I spent Thanksgiving with his family (my family) and tried hard to envision what having him there would be like. And this year, I found out. Pure joy!

Ann

Bigger than Us

When we make everything about us, our focus becomes narrow and self-serving. Rather than having praise reports, we start having pity parties.

Ann-Maria Benton

Let us reflect on Joseph's life a little more. When he was young, he had a dream symbolizing his family bowing down to him. And while his dream was a sneak peek into his future, it was just a snapshot, not a roadmap detailing how he would get there – he did not see anything about a pit or a prison.

As it happened though, Joseph was thrown into a pit by his brothers on one occasion, then falsely accused of rape and thrown into prison on another, before being invited back into the palace. Yet, despite his considerable hardships, Joseph remained faithful to serving God, operating as a man of foolish faith instead of complaining about the problems.

Even today, we must acknowledge this compelling lesson, because the enemy will always throw up problems and challenges in our lives to distract and discourage us. To persuade us to feel sorry for ourselves and make it all about us. But God wants us to know that His plan for our lives is so much bigger than us!

This was one of the first things Willie explained to me. Although we loved each other deeply and knew God had brought us together, His plan for doing so was bigger than us. And while I agreed, conceptually, the true test of my belief came when things did not look the way I had hoped or expected.

Being honest, I initially envisioned God using us mightily *after* Willie got out of prison. How much easier it would have been for us to be *together*, sitting on a stage, or doing a Facebook Live, talking about where he *used to be.* Surely, God's plan could not possibly include denial of parole and adding another two years to his sentence. Ugh. But it did!

Yet, during Willie's final two years, I believe we both ministered and shared the goodness of God more than previous years, as we truly took our eyes off our situation and placed our complete focus on Him. No longer *obsessed* with Willie getting out.

In hindsight, because it was bigger than us, I am thoroughly convinced those additional two years were necessary if it allowed Willie to speak with, encourage, pray with, or mentor *one* lost brother. One lost soul.

Similarly, I am thoroughly convinced that if it took for me to finally share openly about where my husband was so others could find hope, the two additional years were necessary because it was bigger than us.

For the more I shared our testimony, the more I shared about where my husband was, the more I shared about God's redemptive power, the more I shared about God's sovereignty, and the more I shared about the foolish faith He had given us, the more I became free. The more I became *empowered* to boldly advocate for the psychological and spiritual freedom of others. To pray for those who needed a miracle. To encourage those who would dare to have faith that seemed foolish. To reassure those who were feeling isolated by lack of support from others.

As a matter of fact, when I initially learned that Willie was being denied parole for two more years, I was in Florida getting ready to preach to a church full of women. When I received the news, I wanted to call it off. I wanted to go curl up in a corner somewhere. The *last* thing I wanted to do was preach about hope, faith, and the like.

However, I quickly concluded that God, in His sovereignty, already *knew* where I would be when I got the news and trusted me to encourage others, despite what I was going through. To exercise foolish faith. The kind of faith that believed the parole board did not have the final say. To believe that God was still in control.

Praise the Lord, He spoke a powerful sermon through me. Several women were saved, healed, and set free that night because I pressed forward, knowing it was bigger than me. Trusting God to do in me what only He could do.

Interestingly, not long afterwards, Willie and I got married. Right where he was. Right there in the prison. Initially, we had planned to have a small wedding while he was inside, then have a "real wedding" when Willie got out. But guess what? There was no *realer* wedding than the magnificent one we had.

Truly, we were blessed to have Chaplain Moss give us her blessing and help make the arrangements. We were blessed to have our married friends, Deon and Leah, who are both pastors, officiate our ceremony. And we were blessed to have our parents in attendance, to have beautiful pictures that captured the wonderful moments. Yet, the blessings did not stop there.

You see, I had told God (before meeting Willie) the next time I got married, I wanted four things:

1. The man who *chose* me
2. The man *I* chose
3. The presence of the Holy Spirit
4. A *slamming* dress - all the ladies will get that last one.

As God is my witness, all my requests were granted by the Lord. Now that is a *real* wedding! There were tears, laughter, exchanging of vows, and quality time spent together with our family afterward. A mini reception of sorts.

Later, Willie was approached by several inmates and Department of Corrections' staff who heard about our wedding and were moved. Several inmates were inspired to obtain their marriage license. It was so much bigger than us.

God's plan is never about one, but He will use the *one*. The one who is obedient. The one who trusts Him. The one who makes him/herself available.

Satan also knows the impact of *one.* He knows if he can deceive a mom or a dad, he can assault an entire family. If he can manipulate one pastor, he can destroy an entire church. If he can mislead a president, he can bring down a nation.

No doubt, Satan knows the power of one; and if he can discourage or distract us, the problem becomes a lot bigger than us. What we do or do not do impact so many others.

God's plan is to reach an entire family, a generation, a culture, and a nation. His goal is many, but His strategy is through one. One obedient person. One person who realizes it is bigger than himself/herself.

You are that one. God wants to use you to break family cycles and patterns. To do what has never been done in your community. To be the light in your dark workplace environment. To have faith that seems foolish to those around you.

It is time to stop focusing on you because it is so much bigger than you!

Although I initially told Ann the purpose for our union was bigger than us, I received a deeper revelation when I was denied parole. Prior to being set off, it was about me and Ann. About us getting to know each other. About us writing letters to the parole board. About us fasting and praying for me to be released. Yep, it was always about us and our plans. Not in a bad way, but in a narrowly focused way.

In hindsight now, I can *see* and understand more about what God wanted to do in me and through me for the next two years, if I could only take my eyes off my own situation and begin to seek the bigger picture.

If not for the set off, for example, I probably would not have been motivated to publish *Men of Hope: Straight Talk From Lifers*. I would not have become acutely aware of the numerous men with incredible gifts, stories, advice, and testimonies to share. I would not have witnessed the great stir it caused when we released it. I would not have been able to accommodate a well-known judge who purchased several copies to distribute to at-risk juveniles.

During the same two years, Ann *finally* released a book she had been (talking about) working on for years: *Pregnant with a Promise – Get Ready to Push!* A book I believe she had been waiting for me to be released before she could confidently encourage others to birth their promise *after* she had birth hers.

Nevertheless, the Lord showed me that she (we) was birthing more than one promise. For He was doing so many amazing things in our lives, despite where I was. He was blessing us. He was blessing our ministry. He was blessing her relationships, helping her to release some and embrace others, as she was traveling and preaching around the world.

So, I strongly encouraged her to get back to writing the book. After which she began making great progress, then she stopped writing again because she admittedly did not know how to encourage those who had given birth when it felt like she was still laboring.

Fortunately, God helped me remind her of the numerous promises she had already birthed, including her relocation to Georgia – that was a big one! Being encouraged, thinking of the numerous people who needed to birth what God placed in them, she buckled down and completed a phenomenal book.

I cannot count the numerous testimonies we have heard from those who learned they had a powerful promise within them and those who needed that push to nurture and birth what God placed in them. Initially, Ann got stuck in the writing process because she was focused on self. But when she focused on the bigger picture and what she believed God would do through the book, she was able to complete it; and it changed many lives.

Truth be told, if I had been released when we wanted me to be, that book would probably not had been written because we would have been too busy doing other things. Distracted. So, we are grateful that God's plan prevailed because it is bigger than us.

Understanding all this now, be encouraged that the tough season you are in is bigger than you. Bigger than your situation. Bigger than you can imagine. Because someone somewhere is banking on you to make it through, overcome, speak up, and complete what you started. Your obedience and perseverance will empower them to walk in what God has for them.

Rest assured that God has given you everything you need to make it through, because you are paving the way for others. It is bigger than you!

It is our prayer that through our sharing you will be encouraged to keep believing God's promise, no matter how foolish your belief may seem to others. No matter what others may say or think.

Some people did not believe we were hearing from God regarding our union. We could imagine them getting wind of the parole denial. They might have said, "How can this be God? You all should give up on this dream of being together."

We are so glad God's plan was bigger than us, as we continued to have *foolish* faith. We believed what God told us and showed us. And here we are, having the privilege and honor to touch the lives of many, through our testimony.

Keep the faith! No matter how foolish it seems. God will do what He says, and He will do it through you, if you continue to *believe*.

Remember, it is bigger than you!

Closer to Home for Christmas (December 2018)

I was still at the transitional center. However, I was able to go home for a few hours. Ann made our first Christmas together so very special. We had the greatest gift of all, each other!

Willie

Favor and Protection

My entire prison experience was a blessing to me for one reason: *God's favor and protection.* It kept me and sustained me even before I knew Him, and it was undoubtably because people were praying for me. Praying I did not fall victim to the drug abuse, gambling, senseless violence, or unlawful sexual activities happening behind the walls.

Glory be to God, my story is not a negative and horrific one, even though my first few years were spent in some of the worst prisons in Georgia and I was surrounded by every kind of craziness imaginable. And I shutter to think how different my experience could have been if not for Him – I'm telling you; God's favor and protection is *real*!

Take my first hair-raising, close-call experience for instance. After being sentenced to serve two consecutive Life sentences, I was transferred to a notorious prison for young adult offenders known as Alto (or the Toe). Because of my lengthy sentence, I was placed on maximum security and locked down on the third floor of an oppressive building, in a one man cell the size of a decent closet. And every time I left my cell, once a day for recreation, and once a day for a shower, I was handcuffed and shackled.

As it happened, one of the guys I killed had an uncle housed there and assigned to work as an orderly in the same unit I was locked down in. He was a huge, muscled guy, and whenever I left my cell in restraints, he was roaming around unrestrained and often unsupervised. While he never said anything to me, he did have strong words with my co-defendant, making it clear that he was waiting for the right opportunity to exact revenge.

Even though he could have easily attempted to pick me up and throw me over a rail or push me down the stairs to my untimely death, he opted to wait until I was released into general population, where a serious war between the "Miami Boys" and the boys from "Da City" (Atlanta) was underway. Where he would be backed by his boys, have unlimited access to chain-gang weapons, and have a better chance of getting away with it.

But you best believe I had no intention of going out bad! No, I was doing 5,000 push-ups, sit-ups, and squats every other day, preparing for the inevitable showdown.

Nevertheless, the vicious stabbing and beating of a guy from Da City and the subsequent and monumental outcry from his mother prompted the prison officials to lock down the whole facility (which had previously been unheard of) and transfer well known troublemakers to adult prisons. And, yep, you guessed it! Most of the Miami Boys were the first to leave.

So, by the time I was released into general population, in God's perfect timing, the uncle and all his boys were gone. The war was over, and I was able to pursue positive and production things, instead of having to kill someone else or be killed myself. And let me tell you, the opportunities to do great things were endless because of God's *favor* and protection.

You see, even though you rarely heard about it, since Alto was designed for youthful offenders (with overcrowded housing up to 1,700), the educational opportunities were exceptional. I mean, there was a vocational trade building that rivaled Atlanta Area Tech, with every trade available. And since I had already obtained my G.E.D., I was genuinely like a kid at an amusement park. Ready for everything, even though I could only take one trade at a time.

I chose to take up electrical wiring because I have always had a fascination with electricity and electronics, and I will never forget my first couple of days in the class.

The first day was boring, as I was given a bunch of safety videos to watch, which put me straight to sleep. Waking up with a crook in my neck, I hoped there would be more to the class, even though most of the guys were not doing anything constructive, and the instructor was not saying anything – he certainly wasn't teaching.

On my second day, I observed a guy finalizing the wiring for a framed house project that required completion before graduation and glanced at the book he was consulting. After a few hours, I concluded out loud that electrical wiring was easier than I thought – really, I did not think there was much to it, but I was not trying to sound cocky or overconfident.

Surprisingly, the teacher found his voice. "What did you say?" He asked from behind his desk, in a fenced area with dozens of tools.

"I was just saying electrical wiring is easier than I thought."

"Oh, really?" He came out of the cage to stand before me, a skeptical white man looking upon a black teenager. "You think you can do this? You think you can run wire?"

"Yes, sir, I'm pretty sure I can."

"I'll believe it when I see it. Tell you what, take a book with you to look over tonight. And tomorrow, I'll give you chance to show me what you got."

After skimming the book, I struggled to sleep as I kept *visualizing* what I needed to do. Yet, I woke up refreshed and excited. And, yep, you guessed it! I correctly wired that framed house in a matter of hours. On my third day of class, I successfully completed the project reserved for those graduating.

When the teacher saw this, astonished, he ran to get his boss and several staff members to come see it, to come meet me. And from that day forward he embraced me as his protégé and taught me everything he knew, treating me as if I were his son – God bless him and his family forever.

And that was just the beginning, for when I was transferred to Hays State Prison a few years later, God's favor and protection followed me. You see, Hays was a disciplinary prison, but I was not sent there for disciplinary reasons. In fact, of the bus load of guys I arrived with, I was the only one placed in general population instead of I.T.P. (Intense Therapeutic Program) because I was sent there to work maintenance, not because of bad behavior.

Now, get this, when I spoke to my counselor, an older black woman, about being assigned to maintenance, she initially refused to do so because no black men worked that detail. Persisting, I showed her my electrical wiring certificate and eventually persuaded her to do her job and submit my request to the classification committee. They tentatively approved it and scheduled an *interview* with the maintenance staff.

If you understood this, you would be laughing! You see, I was not seeking a job. No, this was a work detail, with no pay, and inmates usually did not interview for such things – you worked where you were *assigned* to work, whether it was digging swamps, breaking rocks, doing laundry, or cooking and cleaning in the kitchen. You did what you were told, no questions asked, unless you wanted to get beat down. Never forget, this was prison!

Still, I was not *trying* to do hard labor, so I went to the interview and found myself sitting before another skeptical white man.

"It says here that you're an electrician, is that correct?" He asked.

"Yes, sir. I am a *certified* electrician."

He grunted and leaned back in his chair, obviously studying me, and I looked right back at him, assessing him. Eventually, he smirked and said, "A certified electrician. Well, tell me this, if I wanted to change the rotation on a three-phase motor, how would I do it?"

"That's easy," I replied, smiling. "Three phase means there are three hot legs. So, to change the motor rotation, all you have to do is switch any *two* of the hot legs."

"Well, I'll be darn, you *are* an electrician!" He paused, then confessed, "More impressive... you looked me in the eye the whole time. I can tell you are a good guy, and we can use your help. Be here first thing in the morning."

Glory be to God, even though I was indeed the first and only black guy assigned to the detail, those guys treated me well, as if they respected my skills instead of seeing my color. Nevertheless, after working with them for over a year, a close friend encouraged me to sign up for the Audio/Visual Repair class he was enjoying. When my request was submitted to the classification committee, it was denied because I already had one vocational trade – I do not think they wanted me to leave maintenance.

But I refused to take no for an answer because, if you remember, I really loved electricity and *electronics*. So, I sent the instructor a typed resume and asked if he could assist me. And assist me, he did! Impressed by the fact that no one had ever sent him a typed resume before, he went to bat for me and had me assigned to him as a vocational aide.

Talk about God's favor and protection! Even though I had not taken the twelve-month course, had not even reviewed the curriculum, the teacher brought me in as his inmate instructor. And I learned so much from this wonderful man in the years I worked for him because he respected the gifts in me and appreciated my love for what he loved.

Truly, I can go on and on with dozens of similar stories. For in addition to receiving several vocational trades, I was also blessed to be involved with a phenomenal program at Shorter College, where their amazing instructors treated us as if we were the best students they ever taught, sharing their invaluable knowledge and experiences with us. I still remember how many of our incredible teachers literally cried when the elimination of the Pell Grant forced them to cancel the program, despite the astounding success of it.

Having walked in God's tremendous protection and favor for years, by the time I met Ann, I had already accomplished a lot and I really had my act together. So, when she asked very direct questions about my activities, I was grateful I had nothing to hide. Nothing to be ashamed of. Nothing to feel bad about. Nothing to cast a shadow of doubt upon me.

In fact, when Ann began visiting and attending various events, she interacted with many, mostly staff members and volunteers, who had known me for years and heard nothing but positive things. Which, of course, solidified my character, verified my good intentions toward her, and evidenced God's favor. Which allowed her to keep moving forward with confidence.

Trust me, I am a living witness of how God can heal, redeem, protect, and use someone while incarcerated. And I want others to know that spending time in prison does not have to be the end of your life. In fact, it can be the beginning. A new beginning. A new opportunity to take advantage of everything positive prison has to offer like I did.

Ann lovingly jokes that no one would want to do a documentary on my life in prison because it would be boring - our society prefers stories overflowing with pain, drama, hysteria, and sensationalism.

However, I disagree with her. I believe my story is worth sharing because there is a mom out there whose teenage son just received a Life sentence. There is a wife whose husband just received 15 *mandatory* years. There is a man whose baby's momma just received 8 years. So on and so on.

And that's why I pray my story inspires you. Trust in God, surround yourself with positive people, spend your time productively, follow the rules, respect the staff, and accept responsibility for what you did or did not do. God's favor and protection will be with you!

Use your gifts and your talents to be a blessing to others. Recognize that while your previous actions and decisions negatively affected others, what you do over the next couple of years can *positively* affect others. Right where you are. Beginning right now.

Real talk, I believe being in prison saved my life, and I was blessed despite being there. So, I woke up each day with a song in my heart and a praise on my lips because I knew God *loved* me. I knew He *still* had a plan for my life. And I *knew* His favor and protection was real!

Ann

As God's daughter, I initially thought His demonstration of favor and protection over my life would always *feel* good. But I have since learned that God's favor can often attract negativity. Sometimes, having favor can cause people to dislike you, become jealous of you, and misunderstand you.

Similarly, while His protection is *always* for our good, it may not always *seem* good. Looking back, I can attest to times in my life when God protected me by closing a door, removing a person, or blocking what seemed like a great opportunity. At the time it may have stung, but the result was undoubtably for the best. For my best.

And even though He has a way of bringing us around, I am grateful God does not interfere with our free will. In other words, He will allow us, sometimes with great sadness, to make decisions that will yield difficult repercussions. The fact that He does not override what we do is amazing. Commendable even.

But I know some people who were upset with God because He did not stop them from making a bad choice. As if we can have it both ways. No, we cannot welcome God to take over when we are making a bad choice, only to snatch back the control of our lives when things are going well. Or worse, we cannot steal His glory, for doing in our lives what only He could!

While God will not override our choices; He, in His sovereignty, will intervene because He is omniscient – all knowing. He knows the beginning from the end. He knows what is going to happen tomorrow, next week, next year, and ten years from now. And He knows the plan He has for our prosperous lives. Therefore, when He intervenes, it is due to knowledge He has about our future.

Sadly, I cannot count how many times God stepped in and did what was best for me. Especially during my wild and crazy teen years. I mean, what was I thinking, or *not* thinking, when I unexpectedly became pregnant by a young man I neither wanted to marry nor have children with? How could I be so irresponsible and not protect myself?

I was so disappointed with myself and too ashamed to tell my parents, who would undoubtedly be disheartened. After all, I had just graduated from high school and found a good job, and it seemed like my life was just beginning. Or should I say it now seemed like my life was being ruined?

Thinking about these things instead of praying about them, I made a decision. A tough one. I contacted a clinic and arranged to have an abortion, and I did not tell anyone. Feeling all alone, I drove myself to the clinic and drove myself home.

Afterwards, I did not go straight home because I was in so much pain, emotionally and physically. Pulling into a fast-food restaurant, I climbed into the back seat and cried myself to sleep for a few hours. When I awoke, feeling somewhat better, I finally went home, conducting myself as normal as I could, so no one in my family had a clue.

Surviving, I moved on with my life, not realizing the impact of my decision until I got married, had two sons, and was desiring to have more. Honestly, I do not know why I became pregnant that time because the marriage was not in a good place. I was stressed to the max, and it negatively affected my pregnancy. In fact, while on a weekend getaway, I aborted six weeks into the pregnancy, and it was devastating.

Still, I survived, and I became pregnant again about a year later. Until, on a Sunday morning, as I was standing in a circle, getting ready to lead praise and worship at my church, I felt liquid run down my legs. Blood.

Without saying anything to anyone, I excused myself, went to the lady's room, and immediately discovered I was miscarrying – again! And I was all alone – again!

I do not know why I did not call out for someone, for help, instead of enduring the horrific event by myself. Believe me, I would not wish what I experienced on my worst enemy. Looking back, I believe I was in shock. Or perhaps I was in denial and disbelief. Whatever. Deep down, I was so hurt!

After cleaning up myself, I went back out to my team. We prayed and, right before we hit the stage, I shared with them what just happened. They looked at me in disbelief, probably thinking I had to be out of mind, insisting I sit down somewhere instead of trying to sing.

Determined to move forward, in survival mode, I was not trying to hear that. Sit down? No, way! I was going to do what I came to do and sing. However, when I started bleeding again, my team ignored me, forced me into a seat, and called an ambulance.

Sadly, since my first miscarriage had not been complicated, I underestimated what was happening this time. I was hemorrhaging, losing lots of blood. So, I was rushed to the hospital, and I remained there the entire day and night.

Days later, I realized I was experiencing serious emotions with God. I was not being thankful that I did not bleed to death in a bathroom all by myself. No! I was angry. I felt like He was punishing me. I felt like because I took a life years earlier, this was my repayment. Locking myself in my bathroom at home, I sat on the floor and just wept. For about an hour.

Afterwards I talked to God, and I was honest, doing my best to express the complexity of what I was feeling. Then... He spoke back, directing me to Psalm 115:3. What? I had no idea what that Scripture said. It was not one I had memorized, nor was it one of my faves.

So, I dried my eyes, went to my bookshelf, and grabbed my Bible. At minimum, I expected it to be a Word of comfort, full of mushy gushy words of how much God loves me. But it was not.

Psalm 115:3 says: God is in heaven and He does what He pleases.

What? All of a sudden, an overwhelming peace washed over me as if someone had poured a bucket of warm water on me. And I instantly felt His love. Felt His protection. Felt His forgiveness. Felt His grace and mercy.

In the midst of my pain, I *still* knew God loved me and did *everything* from a place of love. A powerful love that prompted me to forgive myself for what I had done years earlier. An encompassing love that prompted me to deal with my own guilt and shame instead of blaming God. An embodying love that helped me to understand how nothing in my life had ever been as bad or hurtful as it could have been, as a result of the decisions I made, because His protection and favor was always with me. Whether I realized it or not.

To this day, I am not aware of *everything* God did, allowed, or even blocked. But I am positive that God knows best. Initially, I questioned whether our babies may have suffered, had a defect, or maybe I may have died giving birth. Maybe that is why...

Today, I simply thank God for being who He is and for loving me and forgiving me. I thank God for never failing me. I thank God for protecting me, even when I did not realize it.

I thank God that one day, in Heaven, I will be reunited with *all* my babies. And I am looking forward to that.

Like Willie, I believe that God's protection and favor is very real. I believe that He has our best interest at heart. I believe that He knows how to weave every situation in our lives into a beautiful testimony.

I trust God! We trust God!

It is our prayer that through sharing our experiences, you will recognize God's favor and protection in your own life. The way God leads, guides, protects, and intervenes will be different for each person, but His love is the same.

We have learned, more often than not, God isn't doing something *to* us, He is doing it *for* us. To that end, it is important to keep trusting Him, no matter how challenging things might get.

It is God's desire that we would live an abundant life, here on earth. For that reason, He is always overseeing our decisions, for the purpose of guiding us to our purpose in Him.

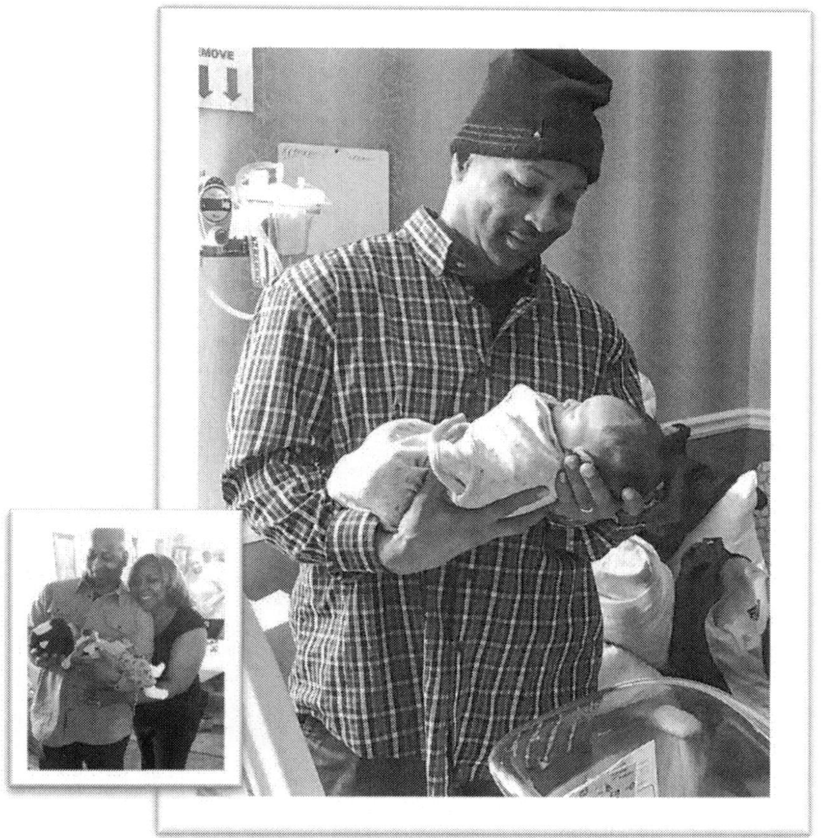

God's Perfect Timing

I am not a person who has regrets. But, one thing I do regret is not being there to watch my son, Marko, grow up. On my birthday in 2019, I received the most wonderful news. Marko and his wife, Britne, were expecting. In December, I was at home to welcome our precious grandson, Ian Alexander, into the world. Thank you, Lord.

Willie

BeYOUtiful

God has given you everything you need to be you and nothing to be someone else.

Ann-Maria Benton

As God's children, we are all created in His image, and I am grateful it does not mean we all look alike or have the same personality. Thank God for uniqueness and diversity. For when embraced and cherished, it makes relationships, groups, and teams vibrant and stronger. Certainly, more colorful.

Willie and I often talk, laugh, and even debate the differences between men and women. And it is crazy how much alike yet different we are. I, for example, am more of a talker while he is more of a listener. Like the average man, he also desires to fix a thing while I am more inclined to feel a thing.

Even knowing this about us, I am careful about imposing generalities and stereotypes because I know some men who like to talk and some women who prefer to listen. Some men who prefer to feel a thing and some women who prefer to fix a thing.

That's why it is important to *know* yourself and always be yourself. For if we are not confident in our uniqueness, we will strive to be a copy of someone else, especially since it is too easy to fall into the "comparison" trap.

Make no mistake about it, comparison is a thief, a divider, and a destroyer, a sure-footed path to a lose-lose scenario. You see, if I compare myself to someone and conclude I am better or smarter, I open the door to a spirit of pride. And I invite the opportunity to put someone down while uplifting myself.

On the flip side, if I compare myself to someone and conclude I could never be as smart, successful, or attractive; I am basically believing God somehow made a mistake when He created me. Believing the clay knows better than the Potter.

Neither conclusion is correct. More importantly, neither one is healthy, optimistic, or beneficial.

Comparison can also lead to competition if we are not careful. Competition, in turn, may cause us to strive to be better at someone else's gift, rather than embracing and cultivating our own. Can you imagine attempting to walk better in someone's shoes than that person? Yet, that is exactly what happens when we attempt to do what someone else was called and chosen to do. When we work harder to fulfill someone's vision than we do our own.

I initially learned a lot about this subject when my family moved from the West Indies to New York. Since I was eight years old at the time, I attended grade school and high school in Brooklyn; and as you can imagine, I grew up exposed to all kinds of trends. Everything from Gazelle glasses to belt buckles spelling my name, from Adidas sneakers to Gloria Vanderbilt jeans – yes, I know, I am dating myself.

Believe me, it was difficult to fit in with my Island accent, as kids teased me about it at first. Yet, succumbing to the pressure to be cool, fashionable, and tough, I eventually became a socialite and was always surrounded with my crew. In fact, you would very seldom find me alone because being around people, being the center of attention, validated me. Defined me. I looked to others for my self-worth and value since I did not know who I was or who I was created to be. I had no idea what I was created to do.

Most of the people I hung around did not know I was insecure, but I was. They did not know my self-esteem was low, but it was. Yeah, I knew how to put up a good front, smiling and laughing a lot. Laughing to keep from crying most of the time. Doing whatever I believed was necessary to be accepted and liked. To stay the life of the party.

Fortunately, as I began to mature in my Christian faith, I desired to learn more about who God said I was and *unlearn* a lot of who others had defined me to be. That is, I was transitioning from the party scene to the church scene.

Still far from perfect though, becoming an active member in a prominent church positively impacted my Christian growth, as the teaching was amazing, and my family was surrounded by a wonderful community of brothers and sisters.

For the first time in years, my life was on the right track, and everything was wonderful until...

Until I had sex with someone I was not married to. Even though we both were single, consenting adults, sex outside of marriage was not permissible in leadership. And I knew it. I also knew there would be consequences and repercussions *when* (not if) it came up.

Yet, when questioned about it, I told the truth and was subsequently stripped of my leadership position. Which was fine since I do believe people in high positions should be held to a higher standard than those we are called to lead.

What I did not expect, however, was how people I had been close to swiftly judged and condemned me after rumors were inappropriately circulated. One day I was being congratulated because my first book was gaining traction, the next day I was being treated as an outcast. One day people were seeking me for prayer and spiritual counseling, the next day they were looking like they wanted to burn me at the stake.

From experience, I learned the term *Church Hurt* is very real. It's when people attend or join a church and experience situations that hurt, rather than heal.

Sadly, anyone, like myself, who struggled with identity issues is a prime candidate for church hurt. Why? Because we place more emphasis on the people than we do on God. We look for people to heal and validate us more than we look to God. And when we run into other people who are hurt, insecure, or controlling, it is only a matter of time before our hurt collides with theirs. Only a matter of time before disaster strikes.

Like most people who experience church hurt, I wanted to *run*. Yep, I wanted to pack up and leave because I felt rejected! But God made it clear I was not to leave wounded. Doing so would allow my pain to become my luggage, which would be unpacked somewhere else if not handled with care.

So, I remained for as long as it took for God to heal me. For as long as it took to get over the disappointment of being misunderstood. For as long as it took to finally embrace who I truly was (flaws and all) and seek how God wanted to use my gifts.

Looking back now, while I could have done things differently, I realize God allowed things to unfold the way they did for me to learn who I was in Him and to prepare me for what He would do next. To prepare me for the Promised Land and my wilderness experience. To prepare me for Willie. To prepare me to be me.

More than ever, I understood that we all must arrive at the place where we are emboldened by and are unapologetic about our uniqueness. And we must desire to connect ourselves with people who see us and appreciate us for who we are, not who they want us to be.

You may wonder how I *knew* Willie was the man God had for me. Well, among other things, he has never asked me to be anyone or anything other than myself. Quite frankly, it was difficult for me to believe at first, but he *consistently* embraced who I am in every situation and in every way. Every day! And that has done more for me and my healing than he may ever know.

People are often surprised when they discover I am a natural introvert. But I am. Which means a lot of my encouragement and affirmation comes from within. That's why being in a one-man cell didn't bother me. No, as long as I had a pen and some paper, I was cool. More importantly, I was free. Free to write and express myself. Free to create my own world and escape reality. Free to discover who I was and love what I saw when I looked in the mirror every day.

Moreover, once I developed a *relationship* with God, my self-worth and value were fully intact because I knew who He said I was. And I thank God for his great assurance because I was immersed in a system filled with labels, starting with an inmate number used to identify you.

If nothing else I learned that labels make a huge difference, consciously or unconsciously. Being at Hays State Prison solidified this important lesson years ago. Designed as a disciplinary prison, there was a behavioral classification system in effect, wherein the worst men (bo' hogs) were housed in E-Building and the best men were housed in A-Building. In general, good behavior allowed men to systematically move from E-Building up the line to A-Building.

Imagine at least 96 men being packed up and moved at the same time from one building to the next, progressing or digressing, according to their behavior the last 90 days or so. Talk about crazy!

Even crazier was how most of the men behaved according to what building they were in. When housed in E-Building, most men behaved as predators, lest they become prey. But move that same man to A-Building and he would act like a saint because he did not want to go back to the jungle.

Similarly, most guys had this thing about being called an inmate or a convict, wherein an inmate was considered soft and obedient, while a convict was considered hard and rebellious. Funny thing, people often asked me if I were an inmate or a convict. My response: neither.

Understand this, I am the son of the Most High God. And he has forgiven me of all my sins. So, why in the world would I forever identify myself with the mistakes I made and the crimes I committed? Instead of letting the past stay in the past, why would I let anyone label me?

Call me what you want to, I promise I will not answer if you call me the wrong thing. I promise I will not get upset if you call me anything, including a racial slur, other than who I am.

Once you know who you are in Jesus Christ, once you know how He died on the cross for you, none of that petty stuff should matter! Once you know you have been *redeemed*, what else matters? Once you know you are loved by an Amazing Father in heaven, what else could possibly matter?

Really, if you did not create me, if you did not save me, if you did not sustain me, if you do not even know me, *why* should I *care* about what you think about me? Why should I care what you say about me, especially when you are talking behind my back?

Seriously, think about it! Why do we give people so much power over us? People who are not paying our bills. People who are not there for us in our times of trouble or sorrow. People who are not and never will be perfect themselves. People who are just *people*.

Over the years, Ann and I have enjoyed deep conversations about these things as I gave her permission to be herself and promised to always be myself – what you see in me is what you get. Period.

While we are not perfect, by God's grace we are perfect for each other. Over six years later, we are still *learning* and *growing* in it. Still thanking God for the many ways He has blessed us and our families – if He doesn't do anything else, He has already done enough, securing us in Him. Glory be to God.

It is our prayer that through our transparent sharing, you will seek God to truly know and embrace your uniqueness. Embrace everything about who you are, flaws and all, the good and the bad.

Do not get caught up in comparing and competing – that is a colossal waste of time. Do not change to fit other's expectation of you because some people will only connect with you if you are being who they want you to be instead of being your true self.

Seek your worth and value from God. If someone hurts you, do not allow what they did to alter who you are – never stop being you! Release the hurt before it consumes you. Release it to God, and He will give you peace. A peace and a joy that surpasses all understanding.

We pray God will show you His amazing plan for you. Your incredibly unique journey. And when He does, we pray you will become confident in being you!

Be YOUtiful!

Tried and True

Trials show that your faith is genuine. It is being tested as fire tests and purifies gold - though your faith is far more precious than mere gold. So, when your faith remains strong through many trials, it will bring you much praise and glory and honor on the day when Jesus Christ is revealed to the whole world.

1 Peter 1:7 (NLT).

More Foolishness

We did not stop praying when Willie came home. We did not stop worshipping and praising God either. We did not stop believing in, trusting in, and depending on Him. No, if anything, our life with Him *intensified.*

Smiling at the memory, I cannot adequately describe what it was like to worship with Willie by my side the very first Sunday. What it was like when the worship team sang an awfully familiar and fitting song, Travis Greene's *You Made a Way.*

Tears streaming down our faces, we belted out these lines: "And we are standing here today only because You made a way." We probably blew the ears off everyone sitting in front of us, as we were making a joyful noise. For all the naysayers criticizing "chain-gang religion", let me tell you, our praise was real because our God is real! Our Lord and Savior, Jesus Christ, is worthy and deserving of our praise.

What had become my church family, welcomed Willie with open arms. Loving him before they met him, many of them had been praying with me, supporting me, and exercising foolish faith for his release with me. At times when I may have doubted or felt discouraged, they were there. They surrounded me. Cried with me. Held my arms high when my hands tried to droop to my side.

Thus, our answered prayers were their answered prayers. And they were ecstatic for us, enthused by what was obviously a colossal move of God. Excited to see what He would do *next* in our lives and their lives.

As for us, we were praying and believing God would bless us with a house. You see, even though I was staying in a lovely apartment and had done my best to make it our home, Willie's name was not on the lease. And it may not have been possible to add him to it since they would want to run a background check – you would be surprised how difficult it is for "returning citizens" to find a place to live.

Since the last thing we wanted to do was live in fear of someone finding out my husband was living with me - sounds crazy right? - we immediately began looking at houses. Small houses, large houses, houses that needed a lot of TLC. Houses closer to Atlanta. Houses closer to Florida. So many houses.

There were too many options, and we could not decide what would be best for us, especially since Willie was eager to show off the construction skills he'd acquired over the years – I was not trying to live in the midst of his renovation project.

One thing we did agree on, however, was that we needed to be on one accord. For it did not make sense to move into any house that one or the other was not at peace with. Being honest, it was more me than Willie because, after living in a two-man cell with a practical stranger for years, his standards were not too high. Anything would be better than what he came from, according to him.

Interestingly, there was one subdivision Willie had his eye on because the houses were moderately priced and close to our current neighborhood. We had looked at the houses several times, and I was not feeling the place because all the homes had one-car garages. Do not ask me why, but I really wanted a two-car garage so Willie could have a workshop. In fact, I wanted it more for him than he wanted it for himself.

We stopped visiting that subdivision for a while and started looking at other ones with gorgeous homes... houses bigger than what we needed. But after ogling and googling over expensive homes one day, we prayed and decided we wanted a home that would not enslave us to debt. We believed God had ministry work for us to do. We would travel. We would be a blessing to others, yet we could not do that if we were in debt to a big fancy house. Bound by worldly possessions.

Having settled it in our hearts, I had thought we were on one accord until, while we were out driving one day, Willie suggested we visit the neighborhood with the one-car garages. To be honest, I was not interested. However, instead of replying indignantly, I stared out the passenger window and rolled my eyes, thinking: *Why are we even wasting time with this neighborhood?*

It was a good thing Willie could not read my mind as we pulled in, immediately noticing that several new homes were being erected. Parking in front of the first nearly completed one we saw, noting that it was unlocked, we entered it and assessed the layout. It was nice, except for the one-car garage.

Overall unimpressed, as I was exiting the house ready to get in the car and leave, I looked across the way and... I did a double take. Were my eyes deceiving me, or was there indeed a house with a two-car garage being built up there?

I pointed it out to Willie, and even though I was tempted to run up the street, I patiently waited for my husband to drive us there. And sure enough, there was a two-car garage home being built. The only one in the *entire* neighborhood. In the perfect location. Unbelievable!

Stepping inside, I instantly fell in love with the amazing floor plan. The layout was great. And, yes, it had a two-car garage. Standing in the unfinished kitchen, I held my stomach, as tears welled up in my eyes, and looked at Willie. "I *feel* like this is *our* home," I declared.

Like Mary, I felt a baby leap on the inside. Having written the book, *Pregnant with A Promise*, I knew exactly what it felt like when something miraculous had been conceived, a spiritual baby. I knew what it felt like when God was doing something remarkable and amazing. Something extraordinary. Something that would forever change my life. Change *our* lives.

"Wow! I have never seen you act this way," Willie said, clearly astounded.

"That's because I have never felt this way about a home."

Believing the house was ours for the taking, we immediately contacted the builder, put in an offer, and placed a deposit. While we were trusting God, we were working with Inspire Loans, and we thought it was cool. Until the lender could not get the numbers right – we loved the house but were not trying to pay too much down, pay too much for closing costs, or pay too much more on a monthly mortgage than we were currently paying for rent.

Sadly, the deal fell through, and the house, our home, was being placed back on the market. A realtor mentioned something about contacting Faith, another lender; but to be honest, I was struggling with what was happening. Struggling with our promise, our spiritual baby, being aborted. Struggling with losing our home before we even got it.

When Willie and I pray about a thing, we always (often reluctantly) ask God to close the door on the opportunity if it is not of Him. And it appeared He was doing just that. Understandably, I was sad, confused, and disappointed. But I would live, and I would get over it, as long I did not drive by the house and see a *sold* sign in the yard – that would have broken my heart!

As we were accepting our grim reality, we received a phone call from Inspire Loans. Reconsidering some things, they believed they could get us into the house, but we were no longer confident in them. No longer inspired by them. Thus, when the helpful realtor reminded us to contact the other lender, whose name is Faith, we did.

Are you getting this? There is a *real-life* message here. Too often we are looking to be inspired. We are looking for something to appeal to our emotions and make us feel giddy. But to please God we must have faith (Hebrews 11:6). Inspiration is temporary and often about us, while faith is all about God.

When we contacted Faith, the interaction with her was genuinely pleasurable, a thousand times better than our experience with the other lender. Seriously, she was a blessing straight from heaven. Not only was she making the process easy, but we loved and appreciated the numbers she brought to the table, loved and appreciated the way Faith was making this thing happen.

Still, we had options and we needed to decide something fast. In hindsight, it seems like a no-brainer, yet it wasn't until after we prayed about it that God led us to go with Faith – we needed to continue walking in foolish faith. In doing so, Faith made it happen, in God's perfect timing. Not only did we get the numbers we desired, with a mortgage less than the apartment's rent, but we also received a hefty refund after closing costs and legal obligations were met. Can you believe it?

Unspeakably grateful, when we moved into our brand-new home, we walked around the entire property, inside and outside, and dedicated it to God. For it was because of the foolish faith He planted in us that Willie came home, and we were now the proud owners of our own home. Free to continue to live a life of foolish faith instead of living in fear.

And get this! Remember how I described when I was standing in the kitchen for the first time, it was like a baby leaped in my belly, reminded of how Baby Jesus leaped in Mary's belly? Remember how I *knew* in my spirit we were standing in our home? How I knew we had conceived and was about to give the same type of spiritual birth I wrote about in *Pregnant With A Promise*?

Well, you are not going to believe this – we keep telling you that we could not make it up if we tried! – but our new home is on Mary Avenue. Let that one sink deep into your spirit for a moment.

Another thing, when we spoke with the construction manager on closing day, we inquired about our home being the *only* two-car garage in the entire subdivision. He confessed it had been a mistake and was not sure how plans for it slipped through. But he had been instructed to build it anyway, and that is what he did.

Willie and I *know* how it slipped through because we know and serve the Master Builder. We know Who is writing our story. Who knows the plans He has for us and our lives. Who is incredibly faithful and encourages us to have foolish faith in Him. Who encourages us to trust in Him, depend on Him, and believe in Him no matter how things may appear. No matter what others may say or think.

Willie

Wow! I am sitting at my first workstation as we wrap up our story. Sitting before my first laptop computer. Sitting in my first home. Real talk, thinking about all the firsts, I could literally cry with authentic and unrestrained joy, happiness, peace, and success.

Of all the firsts, however, the most remarkable and amazing one concerned my son and daughter-in-love, who had been saying for years they were not planning to have any kids, ever. Ever! Since they are a happily married, wonderful, loving, and supportive couple who would make terrific parents, I was always baffled by this.

More precisely, I often wondered if their decision had anything to do with the fact that I practically abandoned my son, by default, when I was incarcerated. While this will always be my biggest regret, not being there for him, I have apologized, forgiven myself, and released it. And I believe he has done the same thing because we have a great relationship.

Still, I could not help but wonder…

Until I was blessed to go home, released from the transitional center a few days before my birthday – talk about a B-day celebration! Well, it only got better when I received a phone call from my son on my birthday and was informed that I was going to be a grandfather.

Glory be to God, I could have fainted. I could have died and gone to heaven, except I wanted to be there for this wonderful experience. I wanted to bask in this unexpected blessing. Yes, I wanted to enjoy it as much as possible.

Like kids, Ann and I rolled around the floor like kids, crying and laughing, after we received the news. Why? Because we genuinely love them and were so happy for them. Knowing them, having said so many prayers for them, we were extremely glad they were being blessed in the ultimate way.

Plus, Ann and I recognized how perfect God's timing was. Wherein we could have received this news while I was still locked up and would not have been there to truly experience this blessing with them. But as God would have it, both Ann and I were there when our first grandson was born. And no words can describe how it felt to hold him in my arms, immediately noticing how he looked just like me, admiring the dimples he inherited from me.

Whew! I can cry right now thinking about standing next to my son as he held his son, admiring the comfortable and competent way he did it, while our wives smiled at us. Three generations of men. Three generations of blessings. Three generations of answered prayers.

When I went to prison, I should have lost everything. But God redeemed me, and He redeemed the time. You see, I had one son back then, now we have three sons. Now we have a granddaughter and a grandson. And we adore them all and recognize they are marvelous blessings. Incredible gifts.

We always pray God will bless our kids and grandkids above and beyond what He is doing for us. We want our floor to be their ceiling. We want our highest point in life to be the springboard for their success. More importantly, we want them to operate and live in a foolish faith.

We pray sharing what God can and will do when we have faith in Him encourages you.

Be encouraged that what God has for you is for you. Be encouraged that the rest of your life is the best of your life. For God can do more in the next two years than He has in the last ten years, redeeming the time, if you trust Him.

If God can take someone who spent thirty-one years in prison, bless him with his soul mate, bless us with grandkids, bless us with great jobs, bless us with nice and reliable vehicles, bless us with our own beautiful home, and bless us with an incredible story of foolish faith; you best believe He can do it for you. And He wants to do it for you.

Do not get caught up on your past mistakes. Do not get stuck in would haves, could haves, or should haves. Instead, thank God for life now! Believe God can turn your situation around. Believe that He is for you. Believe He wants to bless you.

Believe! And do your part - trust Him! Keep trusting Him. Especially when things look the opposite of what God says. That is when He wants us to demonstrate foolish faith. Faith that He can and will do what seems impossible.

Are you ready to have foolish faith? We did and His blessings keep coming. Thank you, Lord!

Two Peas in a Pod

As a minister, people who don't know me personally often think I am serious most of the times. But those who really know me, know I like to cut up. No one knows this more than Willie. I'm the one who likes to hide in dark places and jump out, making weird noises in an attempt to scare Willie. It never works, but it often leaves us laughing until our stomachs hurt. Willie knows I can be weird, funny, serious, dramatic, complex, moody, loving, compassionate, passionate and everything in between, and he loves me just the way I am.

Ann

This is Us

Individually, we are not perfect. But together, we are perfect.

The Bentons

Like many of you, we enjoy watching the TV series *This is Us*. If you watch, you know each episode addresses life issues every viewer can relate to. They do not shy away from topics like race, obesity, eating disorders, adoption, drug use, illness, sexuality, rejection, shame, and keeping secrets.

Each week, the members of the Pearson family muddle through identity issues, while being mindful of how their decisions affect the ones they love. When the characters face situations head on, they learn a little more about themselves. However, when the characters avoid the situations, they are robbed of knowing themselves at a deeper level.

They are ever growing and evolving before our eyes. We laugh and cry with them and marvel at the fact that Jack is gone, but not really.

We see their imperfections on display as they try to decipher their unique contribution to the life and family they've been given.

That's us.

Life has dealt us cards that, at times, felt like a losing hand. But, because we kept playing and didn't quit, it turned out to be a winning hand.

Each challenging situation we encounter, we desire to learn the lesson so we can become better, not bitter.

Some people will get us and some won't. And it's okay.

Jesus told the disciples, when they visited a home or town where the people rejected the message, to shake the dust off their feet as they left. Matthew 10:14

The only things collecting dust are things not being used. Things that are inactive. Things, like feet, standing still in a place of non-productivity.

Like the disciples, we refuse to be inactive and collect dust, waiting for people to cosign what God has *already* approved. We lovingly shake the dust off and move forward, staying productive, using our gifts, and testifying about God's goodness.

We've both made decisions in the past that had adverse effects on us and everyone we love. It's our deep desire to face our challenges head on so God's faithfulness, power, strength, and resilience can shine through us.

We want our potholes to warn others. We want our lessons learned to teach others. We want the hurdles we overcome to inspire others. We want our deep love for the Lord and each other to encourage others. We want our obedience to God to influence others.

God has brought us a mighty long way, and we are proud to say *This is Us!* This is who we are, unapologetically, and undeniably.

We thank you for the honor and privilege of sharing our story with you. We did our best to bring our authentic selves to this book, while giving God the glory and praise He deserves.

Nothing in this book is about what we did; it's about what God did and will continue to do when we exercise a faith that seems foolish at times.

We pray you are inspired to have foolish faith and trust God to step out of the boat, even if you do it afraid and alone. If God calls you out, He will be with you - He won't let you down, or let you drown!

Stay tuned. There's more to come.

God bless you! Willie and Ann.

#BentonsforLife

Dared to Believe (July 2020)

Here we are, standing in the kitchen where it felt like a baby leaped in my belly a few months earlier. Before we were approved, we walked around our home and decreed it was ours. We had complete faith in God. And He did it. We dared to imagine and God exceeded it.

Ann

Thank You for Helping Us

We desire to strengthen the faith of others by sharing our story and using our God-given gifts to be a blessing. We cannot do it alone. We need your help.

You can help by:

- Writing a book review on Amazon. Let others know how this book has impacted your faith and provided clarity about your own journey.
- Visiting our website, joining our email list, and connecting with us on social media.
- Sharing with others how this book has impacted your faith and/or given you hope.
- Inviting us to speak at your church, events, conferences, etc. We are passionate about reaching the youth, inspiring young adults, encouraging married couples, advocating for inmates (former and current), and helping individuals live a life of freedom!

Thank you in advance!

Meet the Bentons

Born and raised in Atlanta, Willie is a sought-after author whose descriptive and engaging style of writing keeps readers on the edge of their seats wanting more. His ability to combine romance, action, thought-provoking, and inspiring messages in one story is unique and amazing.

At age 17, Willie made a regrettable decision that to the natural eye should have ended his life. But little did he know that God would turn his mistakes around for his good and for God's glory (Romans 8:28).

Ann-Maria (aka the #TruthTeacher) is an ordained Reverend, best-selling author, and transformational speaker. A woman of many talents, she is a former radio host, and a gifted speaker, who interweaves the truth of God's Word, humor, and transparent testimonies to create an atmosphere for authentic and life-transforming encounters. Standing firm on John 8:32, she believes that knowing the truth unleashes freedom, and freedom gives birth to one's full potential.

When not serving in their local church, the couple can be found volunteering at local organizations, mentoring young people, and speaking a message of hope at various events.

Willie and Ann-Maria co-founded Freedom Focused Ministries, co-own their business, Simply Ideal Solutions, LLC, and sit on the Board of Directors for Purpose for Your Life Centre and Red Clay Ministries, Inc.,

Together, the couple has co-authored fifteen books and are passionate about empowering individuals to live a life of freedom and purpose.

The couple has three amazing adult sons, two beautiful grandchildren, and currently reside in Georgia.

To learn more about the Bentons, visit www.freedomfocusedministries.com.

Made in the USA
Columbia, SC
27 October 2024